Everyman's Poetry

Everyman, I will go with thee,
and be thy guide

Robert Herrick

Selected and edited by DOUGLAS BROOKS-DAVIES

EVERYMAN

J. M. Dent · London

This edition first published by Everyman Paperbacks in 1996

Selection, introduction and other critical apparatus
© J. M. Dent 1996

J. M. Dent
Orion Publishing Group
Orion House
5 Upper St Martin's Lane
London WC2H 9EA

Typeset by Deltatype Ltd, Ellesmere Port, Cheshire
Printed in Great Britain by
The Guernsey Press Co. Ltd, Guernsey, C.I.

British Library Cataloguing-in-Publication
Data is available upon request.

ISBN 0 460 87799 2

Contents

CONTENTS

The White Island, or Place of the Blessed   82
To Christ   83   *tetrameter couplets*
Long Life   84
Mora Sponsi: The Stay of the Bridegroom   84
Tapers   84
Christ's Action   84
Sin   85
Another   85   *heroic couplets*
Another   85
To Keep a True Lent   85   *Heterometric*
Clothes for Continuance   86
The Resurrection   87
Coheirs   87
The Number of Two   87
The Rose   87
Baptism   88
Good Friday: Rex Tragicus; Or, Christ Going to His Cross   88   *heroic couplets*
To His Saviour's Sepulchre: His Devotion   89
His Offering, With the Rest, at the Sepulchre   90
His Coming to the Sepulchre   90
Of all the Good Things   91

Notes   92

Note on the Author and Editor

ROBERT HERRICK was born in 1591 in Cheapside, London, to Nicholas, a goldsmith, and Julia (or Juliana). Their seventh child, he was baptised on 24 August. Nicholas died after a fall from a window the following year. Although little is known of the intimate details of Herrick's life (some letters survive alongside the poems, but there are few other records), its broad shape is clear. He was apprenticed to his goldsmith uncle, Sir William, in 1607, but went to Cambridge as a fellow-commoner at St John's in 1613, graduating from the less expensive Trinity Hall in 1617 with his BA (he took his MA three years later). He was ordained at Peterborough in 1623, remaining in London until he went as chaplain to the Duke of Buckingham on the Isle of Ré in an unsuccessful military expedition to support the Huguenots (1627). After his return he was nominated to the living of Dean Prior (covering a large area south east of Dartmoor), where he remained until expelled by the Puritan purge of Anglicans in 1647. He returned to London, where his *Hesperides* was published in 1648. Although he wrote a few other poems, this remained his lifetime's poetic achievement. With the restoration of the monarchy in 1660 Herrick returned to Dean Prior, where he died, at the age of 83, on 15 October 1674.

DOUGLAS BROOKS-DAVIES was born in London and educated at Merchant Taylors' School, Crosby and Brasenose College, Oxford. Formerly Senior Lecturer in English Literature at the University of Manchester and currently Honorary Research Fellow in English there, he is now a freelance scholar. His publications on Renaissance English literature include *Spenser's 'Faerie Queene': A Critical Commentary* (Manchester University Press, 1977); *The Mercurian Monarch* (Manchester University Press, 1983); *Silver Poets of the Sixteenth Century* (Dent, 1992, 1994) and modernised editions of Spenser's *Selected Shorter Poems* (Longman, 1995) and *The Fairy Queen* (Dent, 1996). He was the main contributor to *The Spenser Encyclopedia* (University of Toronto Press, 1990).

Chronology of Herrick's Life

Year	Age	Life
1591		Born to Nicholas, a goldsmith, and Julia (or Juliana) in Cheapside, London; baptised 24 August (siblings William, born 1585; Martha, 1586; Mercie, 1586; Thomas, 1588; Nicholas, 1589; Anne, 1590; William, 1593)
1592	1	7 November, father Nicholas makes will; 9 November, death of Nicholas after fall from house window (?suicide)
1605	14	William Herrick (uncle, b. 1557) knighted

Chronology of his Times

Year	Literary Context	Historical Events
1588	William Morgan's Welsh translation of Bible	Spanish armada
1590	Marlowe, *Tamburlaine* Spenser, *Faerie Queene*, Books 1–3 Sidney, *Arcadia*	
1591	Harington, translation of Ariosto, *Orlando Furioso* Shakespeare, *2* and *3 Henry VI*	Death of Spanish mystic, St John of the Cross; Trinity College, Dublin, founded
1592	Marlowe, *Edward II, Dr Faustus*	Presbyterianism established in Scotland; remains of Pompeii discovered
1593	Shakespeare, *Richard III* Birth of Herbert Death of Marlowe	Act against Jesuits and other 'disloyal persons'; church attendance compulsory in England; London plague
1595	Shakespeare, *A Midsummer Night's Dream* Spenser, *Amoretti and Epithalamion*	
1596	Spenser, *Faerie Queene*, Books 4–6	English (led by Essex) attack Cadiz
1599	Shakespeare, *Julius Caesar* Death of Spenser	Birth of Oliver Cromwell; James VI, *Basilikon Doron* (defending kingly Divine Right)
1603	Shakespeare, *All's Well That Ends Well* Jonson, *Sejanus*	Death of Elizabeth I, James VI succeeds as James I, grants tolerance to Catholics
1605	Jonson, *Volpone* acted (published 1607) Shakespeare, *King Lear*	Gunpowder Plot

Year	Age	Life
1607	16	25 September, apprenticed goldsmith to Sir William
1611	20	Death of Mary, paternal grandmother
1613	22	Released from apprenticeship, enters St John's College, Cambridge. Becomes acquainted with John Weekes (fellow) and Clipsby Crew (to whom he will address poems). Later moves to less expensive Trinity Hall, Cambridge
1617	26	Graduates BA from Trinity Hall
1620	29	Takes his MA

Year	Literary Context	Historical Events
1607	Tourneur, *Revenger's Tragedy*	English settlement in Virginia; Tyrone flees to Rome; land in Ulster given to English and Scottish settlers
1608	Birth of Milton	Telescope invented by Lippersheim
1610	Beaumont and Fletcher, *Maid's Tragedy* Jonson, *The Alchemist*	Bishops fully restored in Scotland; Hudson Bay explored by Henry Hudson
1611	Authorised Version of Bible	Kepler invents astronomical telescope
1613	Shakespeare, *Henry VIII* Death of El Greco	Michael Romanov elected Tsar
1614	Jonson, *Bartholomew Fair*	Logarithms invented by Napier
1616	Webster, *Duchess of Malfi* Folio edition of Jonson's works Deaths of Shakespeare, Cervantes	Richelieu becomes French Secretary of State
1617		Dismissal of Richelieu
1618		Bacon appointed Lord Chancellor; Ralegh executed
1619	Deaths of Nicholas Hilliard, Samuel Daniel	Villiers created Marquis of Buckingham
1620	Bacon, *Novum organum*	Pilgrim Fathers leave Plymouth in *Mayflower*, arrive December, found New Plymouth

Year	Age	Life
1623	32	24 April, ordained deacon at Peterborough, with John Weekes; 25 April, both ordained priests. Herrick now mainly in London, friend of Ben Jonson, among others
1625	34	'Nuptial Song, or Epithalamy, on Sir Clipsby Crew and his Lady' (wedding 7 July)
1627	36	Army chaplain to Duke of Buckingham on anti-Catholic expedition to Isle of Ré
1628	37	Nominated to living at Dean Prior (south east of Dartmoor), Devon
1629	38	Death of Julia (mother); appointed to Dean Prior
1630	39	29 October, becomes vicar of Dean Prior. Writes 'A Pastoral upon the Birth of Prince Charles' (b. 29 May)
1637	46	Death of Ben Jonson; 'Upon M. Ben Jonson'

Year	Literary Context	Historical Events
1621	Burton, *Anatomy of Melancholy*	
1623	Shakespeare, First Folio	Prince Charles fails to secure Spanish marriage; Richelieu made first minister
1624	Massinger, *The Renegado* Middleton, *Game at Chess*	Virginia a Crown colony; Dutch found New Amsterdam
1625	Massinger, *A New Way to Pay Old Debts*	Death of James I, Charles I succeeds, marries French Catholic Henrietta Maria
1626	Sandys, translation of Ovid's *Metamorphoses*	Irish College founded at Rome
1627	Bacon, *New Atlantis*	Propaganda College (*Collegium de propaganda fide*) founded at Rome
1628		Harvey reveals double circulation of blood; Buckingham assassinated; Taj Mahal built
1629		Parliament dissolved by Charles I; English settle Massachusetts
1630		Congregation of English Ladies founded at Munich; Pope disbands Congregation of Female Jesuits; death of Kepler; Gustavus Adolphus invades Europe
1631	Herbert, *The Temple* Death of Donne	English colonisation of Leeward islands
1633	Donne, *Poems* Prynne, *Histriomastix* attacks stage plays	Laud appointed Archbishop of Canterbury; Charles I crowned king of Scotland
1634	Milton, *Comus*	First levy of 'ship-money' (second, 1635; third, 1636)
1637	Milton, *Lycidas*	Rebellion in Scotland after Charles tries to introduce new Prayer Book; John Hampden and 'ship-money'

Year	Age	Life
1643	52	Death of sister-in-law at Dean Prior
1644	53	'To the King, Upon his Coming . . . into the West'
1645	54	'To the King, Upon his taking of Leicester'
1647	56	'To the King upon his Welcome to Hampton Court' (Charles taken there 24 August). Removed from Dean Prior living; goes to London (probably Westminster)
1648	57	*Hesperides; Or, The Works Both Humane and Divine of Robert Herrick, Esq*
1649	58	'The New Charon: Upon the Death of Henry, Lord Hastings' (d. 24 June)
1652	61	Death of Sir William

Year	Literary Context	Historical Events
1640	Death of Rubens	First session of Long Parliament; Stafford impeached
1641	Death of Van Dyck	Stafford executed; Protestants massacred in Ulster
1642	Browne, *Religio medici* Denham, *Cooper's Hill*	Civil War begins; theatres closed until Restoration; death of Galileo
1643		Defeat of Hampden (royalist victory); Solemn League and Covenant between Parliament and Scots
1644	Milton, *Areopagitica*	Defeat of Royalists at Marston Moor; Louis XIV king of France
1645	Waller, *Poems*	Defeat of Royalists at Naseby; Laud executed; Fairfax creates New Model Army
1646	Vaughan, *Poems*	Charles I surrenders to Scottish army at Newark
1647	Cowley, *The Mistress*	Charles sold by Scots to Parliament for £400,000
1648	Paris Royal Academy of Arts founded	Scots begin Second Civil War; defeated by Cromwell at Preston
1649	Milton, *Eikonoklastes*	30 January Charles I executed; England declared free commonwealth
1650	Milton, *Pro populo Anglicano defensio*	Defeat of Scots by Cromwell at Dunbar; Edinburgh Castle surrenders
1651	Hobbes, *Leviathan*	Charles II crowned at Scone; defeated by Cromwell at Battle of Worcester; Charles to France
1652	Death of Inigo Jones	England at war with Dutch; Royalists pardoned
1653	Walton, *Complete Angler*	Cromwell dissolves Long Parliament; made Lord Protector

Year	Age	Life
1660	69	Back to Dean Prior as vicar
1674	83	15 October, death of Herrick; buried at Dean Prior

Year	Literary Context	Historical Events
1658		Death of Cromwell; son Richard succeeds
1660	Dryden, *Astraea Redux*	Restoration of Charles II
1665		Plague of London
1666	Dryden, *Annus Mirabilis*	Fire of London
1667	Milton, *Paradise Lost*	
1671	Milton, *Paradise Regained, Samson Agonistes*	
1673	Dryden, *Amboyna*	Test Act excludes Catholics from offices under Crown
1674	Wycherley, *The Country Wife, The Plain Dealer* Death of Milton	England withdraws from Dutch war

Introduction

When Robert Herrick died in 1674 his long life had spanned the reigns of four monarchs. Born in 1591, he was eleven when, in March 1603, Elizabeth I died. When he was ordained in 1623 the Authorised Version of the Bible was only twelve years old, testament to a church and state whose stability seemed unquestionable, despite the loud rumblings of the puritans. By the time Herrick was in his forties, Charles I's insistence on his absolutist power to override law and the people, together with his queen's Catholicism and the increasingly strident Anglo-Catholicism enforced by Archbishop Laud, were finally leading to the civil war in which those forms of earthly authority so dear to Herrick – king, bishop, priest – were to be challenged and then superseded by a puritan republic committed to the rigours of the individual conscience and the unmediated word of God. When the republic collapsed and the monarchy was restored, together with the Anglican hierarchy and its liturgies, Herrick was nearly 70.

We know few details of Herrick's life. Having read law at least part of the time he was at Cambridge, he was ordained and eventually became vicar of Dean Prior on the south east edge of Dartmoor. When Devon embraced puritanism, he must have felt increasingly isolated, religious alienation (he was clearly a bibulous, easy-going priest with few urgent theological or existential anxieties) reinforcing the homesickness he felt for his native London. And when he was expelled from his living in 1647 (he was replaced by the puritan John Syms), he recorded his intense delight and sense of relief in 'His Return to London'. His wish (and vow) never to return to Devon was, however, broken at his own request: shortly after the Restoration, Herrick was back at Dean Prior, where he remained as vicar until his death.

Herrick published very little before *Hesperides*, and almost nothing after it, so that the volume stands as the supreme monument to his poetic powers and, given his subsequent failure to publish, as his own last word on himself as a poet. It appeared in 1648, and was in effect two books in one. *Hesperides; Or, The Works Both Humane and Divine of Robert Herrick, Esq* is the overall title, and the title page is dated 1648; but some 79 pages before the end is another title page, which reads *Noble Numbers*, with the date 1647. Herrick obviously oversaw the printing of his volume with some care, so that whatever the reason for the discrepancy in dates, with its apparent implication that *Noble Numbers* should precede (rather than succeed) the secular poems that comprise the body of the volume, we have the volume as Herrick intended it. And as such it suggests a progression from profane to spiritual concerns that is common enough in the period.

Herrick's spiritual journey

Hesperides comprises 1,130 secular poems and 272 *Noble Numbers*, and although the order of the individual poems is apparently random, it would be foolish to assume that it is so. Hence in my text I have followed the lead of some previous editors in designating the *Hesperides* poems by H followed by an ordinal number, and *Noble Numbers* with an N and a number, thus enabling the reader to see where the poems fit into the overall volume as Herrick published it, and to see when I have printed adjacent ones. The importance of this information is demonstrated by the proximity of the group of Candlemas poems (H892–4) to the poem 'Julia's Churching, or Purification' (H898): most Anglicans now think of Candlemas (2 February) as commemorating Christ's Presentation in the Temple. For Herrick (as for Catholics and High-Church Anglicans still) it means the purification of the Virgin Mary after Christ's birth (see note to H892). But we would not know that by merely reading the Candlemas poems, for they talk of pies, the Christmas log and evergreen decoration. It takes the Julia poem retrospectively to illuminate them, to show us how the saving of the Christmas log and displacement of old branches by new ones parallel in a gently mythical way the mysterious cyclicity of the woman's body, and its renewal through blessing after the pains and dangers of childbirth.

But why the title *Hesperides*? The name refers to the daughters of Atlas who were given a garden in the far west, where the sun sets, in which were trees bearing golden apples guarded by a dragon. Primarily, then, *Hesperides* is a garden of verses (it was common at the time to pun on poesy and posy, verse and flower). More particularly, it is a garden of verses, many of which were written in the isolation of what Herrick called on more than one occasion 'the

[margin note: Cine R.S.Thomas]

drooping west' of Devon (H77, 713): his garden of the west is not an especially happy place and the poems are his solace from the realities of a rude and uncouth peasantry (H86). More particularly still, back in London after his expulsion from Dean Prior, his thoughts must have reverted to his youth and birth in 'golden Cheapside' (H1028). The phrase seems aglow with nostalgia, and it is. But it also speaks of precise reality: his father, who died when he was one, had been a goldsmith, and Herrick himself had been apprenticed to his goldsmith uncle, Sir William, in 1607. Cheapside is the place where Herrick decided to forego the family trade in gold. Which leads to the further thought that maybe *Hesperides* is a private homage to the shade of his father – an offering of poetic golden apples to replace the more splendid work he had been expected to achieve as a goldsmith.

A grittier, political reality underlay the choice of title, too. The book was dedicated to Prince Charles, whose birth had been greeted by a bright, midday manifestation of Hesperus (H213n.), which thus seemed providentially to recall the mythologisation of his father as Hesperus in Ben Jonson's court masque, *Pleasure Reconciled to Virtue* (1618), and the identification of Britain in court masques, as elsewhere, as the Hesperides. The publication of *Hesperides* was delayed, it seems, until the royalist cause in the civil war was utterly lost. So the volume is an elegy for a lost western kingdom, for an island overseen by the setting sun of waning monarchical authority. It is no accident, then, that *Noble Numbers* ends with Christ's crucifixion and poems on his sepulchre. Bearing in mind Charles I's insistence on the sacredness of his kingship, the swiftness with which the analogy between executed king and crucified Christ sprang into being in 1649, and the apparent hopelessness of his cause (which it required considerable faith to believe in), it is surely the king as well as Christ to whom Herrick, imagining himself at the empty sepulchre, vows: 'I'll thither follow without fear,/And live in hell if that my Christ stays there' (N271).

Herrick sings of loss, of fleeting time, of seizing the day before it passes for ever, of death. In doing so he echoes Catullus, Horace, Ovid and many other classical and later poets. His epigrams (scattered in great numbers through *Hesperides*) imitate Martial in their pithy vulgarity. He also includes panegyrics to the royal family (mainly the king and Prince Charles). At a distance apparently a motley assembly of verses produced by a man familiar with the classics, on closer inspection the poems become more curious and interesting. You have to catch time opportunely, Herrick says to virgins, daffodils and roses. But he also says that when flower-mothers die in childbirth their 'flosculet' (little flower) regenerates them – thus reverting to one of the oldest mythical themes of classical elegy and of Ovid's *Metamorphoses*. And in touching upon this theme he is reinforcing what his explicit references to classical mythology also achieve: not just a recollection of, but a genuine continuity with, the past. When Corinna (named after Ovid's mistress) goes a-maying (H178) and is compared to Flora, she not only 'revives' Ovid's dead beloved but also a long-lost vegetation goddess whose flower festival in ancient Rome occupied late April to early May, thereby including May Day (or its Roman equivalent).

Herrick records in the minutest detail in many of his poems the folk customs of his part of Devonshire. He must, indeed, have thought that he was in a foreign country – and he was: the foreign country that, according to L. P. Hartley (opening of *The Go-Between*, 1953), is the past, where they do things differently. (It still is an isolated part of Devon, about which rumours can occasionally be heard about pagan practices.) Herrick's inquisitive and enquiring eye recognised this continuity with the past, and it prompted in him (as with others at the time) an interest in antiquarianism. Its effect on him was equivalent to the combined effects of antiquarianism and Darwinism on Thomas Hardy, for whom the maypole at the beginning of *Tess of the D'Urbervilles* recalls some old Floralia, thus testifying to the synchronicity of the past with the present, so that geological stratum becomes continuum. Herrick saw the puritans as attempting a vast discontinuity; his poetry affirms continuity. Poems to the king mingle with addresses to flowers and epigrams on adultery because all together combine into an affirmation that, although things change, in another way they never will because the life force is indestructible and therefore in the end institutions can never die. Ovid's Corinna lives; so does Flora; and so, deep in the depths of the countryside and Herrick's imagination, does Oberon, the Fairy King (H293, 443). However much they may wish to, the puritan revolutionaries can't kill him. Native fairy lore had (through Spenser's *Faerie Queene*, various poems and court masques) been associated with an idealised view of monarchy. Herrick takes that view and, with his strange and magical imagination born of an apprentice goldsmith's eye for precise detail (mushroom tables, 'the shine of snails', a dandelion bed), fuses kingship with nature to create a pastoral beyond pastoral where nostalgia for things past becomes the mystery of the particular – that place identified by George Eliot in *Middlemarch* (Ch. 20) as lying on the other side of silence where the squirrel's heartbeat can be heard. In that world, tinselled with moonlight, glittering with kitlings' eyes and imbued with a folk superstition that Herrick well knew to be ineradicable, kings roam at will, released from imprisonment and exile.

DOUGLAS BROOKS-DAVIES

Robert Herrick

from **Hesperides**

H1

The Argument of His Book

I sing of brooks, of blossoms, birds and bowers:
Of April, May, of June, and July-flowers.
I sing of maypoles, hock-carts, wassails, wakes,
Of bridegrooms, brides, and of their bridal cakes.
I write of youth, of love, and have access   5
By these to sing of cleanly-wantonness.
I sing of dews, of rains, and, piece by piece,
Of balm, of oil, of spice, and ambergris.
I sing of times trans-shifting; and I write
How roses first came red, and lilies white.   10
I write of groves, of twilights, and I sing
The court of Mab, and of the fairy king.
I write of hell; I sing (and ever shall)
Of heaven, and hope to have it after all.

H2

To His Muse

Whither, mad maiden, wilt thou roam?
Far safer 'twere to stay at home,
Where thou mayest sit and, piping, please
The poor and private cottages.
Since cotes and hamlets best agree   5
With this, thy meaner minstrelsy,
There with the reed thou mayest express
The shepherd's fleecy happiness,
And with thy eclogues intermix

Some smooth and harmless bucolics.   10
There on a hillock thou mayest sing
Unto a handsome shepherdling;
Or to a girl that keeps the neat
With breath more sweet than violet.
There, there (perhaps) such lines as these   15
May take the simple villages –
But for the court, the country wit
Is despicable unto it.
Stay, then, at home, and do not go
Or fly abroad to seek for woe: 20
Contempts in courts and cities dwell;
No critic haunts the poor man's cell,
Where thou mayest hear thine own lines read
By no one tongue, there, censured.
That man's unwise will search for ill,   25
And may prevent it, sitting still.

To His Book

While thou didst keep thy candour undefiled,
Dearly I loved thee, as my first-born child;
But when I saw thee wantonly to roam
From house to house, and never stay at home,
I brake my bonds of love, and bade thee go,   5
Regardless whether thou well spedest or no.
On with thy fortunes, then, whate'er they be;
If good, I'll smile; if bad, I'll sigh for thee.

H5   **Another**

        Who with thy leaves shall wipe (at need)
        The place where swelling piles do breed:
        May every ill that bites or smarts
        Perplex him in his hinder parts.

H8 **When He Would Have His Verses Read**

        In sober mornings do not thou rehearse
        The holy incantation of a verse;
        But when that men have both well drunk, and fed,
        Let my enchantments then be sung, or read.
        When laurel spirts in the fire, and when the hearth   5
        Smiles to itself, and gilds the roof with mirth;
        When up the thyrs' is raised, and when the sound
        Of sacred orgies flies around, around.
        When the rose reigns, and locks with ointments shine,
        Let rigid Cato read these lines of mine.   10

H9   **Upon Julia's Recovery**

        Droop, droop no more, or hang the head,
        Ye roses almost withered:
        Now strength and newer purple get,
        Each here-declining violet.
        O primroses, let this day be   5
        A resurrection unto ye,
        And to all flowers allied in blood,
        Or sworn to that sweet sisterhood!
        For health on Julia's cheek hath shed

Claret and cream commingled,   10
And those her lips do now appear
As beams of coral, but more clear.

H11   The Parliament of Roses: To Julia

I dreamt the roses one time went
To meet and sit in parliament:
The place for these, and for the rest
Of flowers, was thy spotless breast,
Over the which a state was drawn   5
Of tiffany, or cobweb lawn.
Then in that parley all those powers
Voted the rose the Queen of Flowers –
But so as that herself should be
The Maid of Honour unto thee.   10

H17   Treason

The seeds of treason choke up as they spring:
'He acts the crime that gives it cherishing.'

H18   Two Things Odious

Two of a thousand things are disallowed:
A lying rich man, and a poor man proud.

H20

The Wounded Heart

Come, bring your sampler, and with art
Draw in it a wounded heart,
And dropping here and there:
Not that I think that any dart
    Can makes yours bleed a tear,   5
    Or pierce it anywhere.
Yet do it to this end: that I
                  May by
            This secret see,
          Though you can make   10
That heart to bleed, yours ne'er will ache
                  For me.

H22

To Anthea

If, dear Anthea, my hard fate it be
To live some few, sad hours after thee,
Thy sacred corse with odours I will burn,
And with my laurel crown thy golden urn.
Then, holding up (there) such religious things   5
As were (time past) thy holy filletings,
Near to thy reverend pitcher I will fall
Down dead for grief, and end my woes withal:
So three in one small plat of ground shall lie –
Anthea, Herrick, and his poetry.   10

H29

Love, what it is

Love is a circle that doth restless move
In the same sweet eternity of love.

H34

The Carcanet

Instead of orient pearls of jet,
I sent my love a carcanet:
About her spotless neck she knit
The lace, to honour me or it:
Then think how rapt was I to see   5
My jet enthrall such ivory.

H35

His Sailing from Julia

When that day comes whose evening says I'm gone
Unto that watery desolation,
Devoutly to thy closet gods then pray
That my winged ship may meet no remora:
Those deities which circumwalk the seas,   5
And look upon our dreadful passages,
Will from all dangers redeliver me
For one drink offering poured out by thee.
Mercy and Truth live with thee, and forbear
(In my short absence) to unsluice a tear.   10
But yet, for love's sake, let thy lips do this –
Give my dead picture one engendering kiss.
Work that to life, and let me ever dwell
In thy remembrance, Julia. So, farewell.

H40

The Dream

Methought last night Love in an anger came,
And brought a rod – so whipped me with the same:
Myrtle the twigs were, merely to imply
Love strikes, but 'tis with gentle cruelty.
Patient I was: Love pitiful grew then,   5
And stroked the stripes, and I was whole again.
Thus, like a bee, Love gentle still doth bring
Honey to salve where he before did sting.

H41

The Vine

I dreamt this mortal part of mine
Was metamorphosed to a vine,
Which, crawling one and every way,
Enthralled my dainty Lucia.
Methought her long, small legs and thighs   5
I with my tendrils did surprise;
Her belly, buttocks, and her waist
By my soft nervelets were embraced;
About her head I writhing hung,
And with rich clusters (hid among   10
The leaves) her temples I behung;
So that my Lucia seemed to me
Young Bacchus ravished by his tree.
My curls about her neck did crawl.
And arms and hands they did enthrall,   15
So that she could not freely stir
(All parts there made one prisoner).
But when I crept with leaves to hide
Those parts which maids keep unespied,
Such fleeting pleasures there I took   20
That with the fancies I awoke,

And found (ah me!) this flesh of mine
More like a stock than like a vine.

H50

To Robin Redbreast

Laid out for dead, let thy last kindness be
With leaves and moss-work for to cover me;
And while the wood nymphs my cold corpse inter,
Sing thou my dirge, sweet-warbling chorister!
For epitaph, in foliage, next write this: 5
    Here, here the tomb of Robin Herrick is.

H51

Discontents in Devon

More discontents I never had
   Since I was born, than here,
Where I have been, and still am, sad,
   In this dull Devonshire.
Yet justly, too, I must confess   5
   I ne'er invented such
Ennobled numbers for the press
   Than where I loathed so much.

H52

To His Paternal Country

O earth, earth, earth, hear thou my voice, and be
Loving and gentle for to cover me:
Banished from thee I live, ne'er to return,
Unless thou givest my small remains an urn.

H53

Cherry-ripe

'Cherry-ripe, ripe, ripe,' I cry,
'Full and fair ones, come and buy.'
If so be you ask me where
They do grow, I answer, 'There,
Where my Julia's lips do smile: 5
There's the land, or cherry isle,
Whose plantations fully show
All the year where cherries grow.'

H54

To His Mistresses

Put on your silks and, piece by piece,
Give them the scent of ambergris;
And for your breaths, too, let them smell
Ambrosia-like, or nectarel;
While other gums their sweets perspire,   5
By your own jewels set on fire.

H55

To Anthea

Now is the time when all the lights wax dim,
And thou, Anthea, must withdraw from him
Who was thy servant. Dearest, bury me
Under that holy oak, or gospel tree,
Where (though thou seest not) thou mayest think upon   5
Me when thou yearly goest in procession.
Or, for mine honour, lay me in that tomb
In which thy sacred relics shall have room:

For my embalming, sweetest, there will be
No spices wanting when I'm laid by thee.   10

H57

Dreams

Here we are all, by day; by night, we're hurled
By dreams, each one, into a several world.

H59

His Request to Julia

Julia, if I chance to die
Ere I print my poetry,
I most humbly thee desire
To commit it to the fire:
Better it were my books were dead
Than to live not perfected.

H69

All Things Decay and Die

All things decay with time. The forest sees
The growth and downfall of her aged trees:
That timber tall, which three-score lustres stood
The proud dictator of the state-like wood
(I mean, the sovereign of all plants, the oak)   5
Droops, dies, and falls without the cleaver's stroke.

H72

Upon his Sister-in-Law, Mistress Elizabeth Herrick

First, for effusions due unto the dead,
My solemn vows have here accomplished;
Next, how I love thee, that my grief must tell,
Wherein thou livest for ever: dear, farewell.

H77

To the King, Upon His Coming with His Army to the West

Welcome, most welcome to your vows and us,
Most great and universal genius!
The drooping west, which hitherto has stood
As one, in long-lamented widowhood,
Looks like a bride now, or a bed of flowers   5
Newly refreshed both by the sun and showers.
War, which before was horrid, now appears
Lovely in you, brave prince of cavaliers!
A deal of courage in each bosom springs
By your access. O you, the best of kings,   10
Ride on with all white omens so that, where
Your standard's up, we fix a conquest there.

H78

Upon Roses

Under a lawn, than skies more clear,
Some ruffled roses nestling were
And, snugging there, they seemed to lie
As in a flowery nunnery.

They blushed, and looked more fresh than flowers 5
Quickened of late by pearly showers,
And all because they were possessed
But of the heat of Julia's breast,
Which, as a warm and moistened spring,
Gave them their ever-flourishing. 10

H79 ## To the King and Queen,
Upon Their Unhappy Distances

Woe, woe to them who, by a ball of strife,
Do, and have, parted here a man and wife:
Charles, the best husband, while Maria strives
To be, and is, the best of wives.
Like streams you are divorced; but 'twill come when 5
These eyes of mine shall see you mix again.
Thus speaks the oak: 'Here C. and M. shall meet,
Treading on amber with their silver feet;
Nor will it be long ere this accomplished be.'
The words found true, C.M. remember me. 10

H82 ## To the Reverend Shade of His
Religious Father

That for seven lustres I did never come
To do the rites of thy religious tomb;
That neither hair was cut, or true tears shed
By me o'er thee as justments to the dead,
Forgive, forgive me, since I did not know 5

Whether thy bones had here their rest or no.
But now 'tis known, behold – behold, I bring
Unto thy ghost th'effused offering.
And look: what smallage, nightshade, cypress, yew,
Unto the shades have been, or now are, due,   10
Here I devote; and something more than so:
I come to pay a debt of birth I owe.
Thou gavest me life (but mortal): for that one
Favour I'll make full satisfaction.
For my life mortal, rise from out thy hearse;   15
And take a life immortal from my verse.

H83 Delight in Disorder

A sweet disorder in the dress
Kindles in clothes a wantonness:
A lawn about the shoulder thrown
Into a fine distraction;
An erring lace, which here and there   5
Enthralls the crimson stomacher;
A cuff neglectful, and thereby
Ribbands do flow confusedly;
A winning wave (deserving note)
In the tempestuous petticoat;   10
A careless shoestring, in whose tie
I see wild civility –
Do more bewitch me than when art
Is too precise in every part.

H86

To Dean Bourne, a Rude River in Devon, by which Sometime He Lived

Dean Bourne, farewell. I never look to see
Dean, or thy warty incivility:
Thy rocky bottom that doth tear thy streams,
And makes them frantic, even to all extremes,
To my content I never should behold   5
Were thy streams silver or thy rocks all gold.
Rocky thou art, and rocky, we discover,
Thy men; and rocky are thy ways all over.
O men, O manners, now and ever known
To be a rocky generation!   10
A people currish, churlish as the seas,
And rude (almost) as rudest savages,
With whom I did, and may re-sojourn, when
Rocks turn to rivers, rivers turn to men.

H89

To Laurels

A funeral stone
Or verse I covet none;
But only crave
Of you that I may have
A sacred laurel springing from my grave,   5
Which, being seen
Blessed with perpetual green,
May grow to be
Not so much called a tree
As the eternal monument of me.   10

To Anthea Lying in Bed

H104

So looks Anthea when in bed she lies,
O'ercome or half-betrayed by tiffanies:
Like to a twilight, or that simpering dawn
That roses show when misted o'er with lawn.
Twilight is yet till that her lawns give way –   5
Which done, that dawn turns then to perfect day.

To Electra

H105

More white than whitest lilies far,
Or snow or whitest swan, you are;
More white than are the whitest creams,
Or moonlight tinselling the streams;
More white than pearls, or Juno's thigh,   5
Or Pelops' arm of ivory.
True, I confess, such whites as these
May be delight, not fully please,
Till, like Ixion's cloud, you be
White, warm, and soft to lie with me.   10

Divination by a Daffodil

H107

When a daffodil I see,
Hanging down his head towards me,
Guess I may what I must be:
First, I shall decline my head;
Secondly, I shall be dead;   5
Lastly, safely buried.

H111   # A Lyric to Mirth

While the milder Fates consent,
Let's enjoy our merriment:
Drink, and dance, and pipe, and play,
Kiss our dollies night and day:
Crowned with clusters of the vine,   5
Let us sit and quaff our wine;
Call on Bacchus, chant his praise,
Shake the thyrs' and bite the bays;
Rouse Anacreon from the dead,
And return him, drunk, to bed;   10
Sing o'er Horace, for e'er long
Death will come and mar the song:
Then shall Wilson and Gualtier
Never sing, or play, more here.

H115 ## The Frozen Zone; Or, Julia Disdainful

Whither? Say, whither shall I fly
To slack those flames wherein I fry?
To the treasures shall I go
Of the rain, frost, hail, and snow?
Shall I search the under-ground   5
Where all damps and mists are found?
Shall I seek (for speedy ease)
All the floods and frozen seas?
Or descend into the deep
Where eternal cold does keep?   10
These may cool; but there's a zone

Colder yet than any one:
That's my Julia's breast, where dwells
Such destructive icicles,
As that congelation will   15
Me sooner starve than those can kill.

H118

The Sadness of Things
for Sappho's Sickness

Lilies will languish, violets look ill,
Sickly the primrose, pale the daffodil:
That gallant tulip will hang down his head
Like to a virgin newly ravished.
Pansies will weep, and marigolds will wither,   5
And keep a fast and funeral together
If Sappho droop. Daisies will open never,
But bid goodnight and close their lids for ever.

H126

Upon Scobble. Epigram

Scobble for whoredom whips his wife, and cries
He'll slit her nose. But, blubbering, she replies:
'Good sir, make no more cuts i'the outward skin:
One slit's enough to let adultery in.'

H128

His Farewell to Sack

Farewell, thou thing, time past so known, so dear
To me as blood to life and spirit; near –
Nay, thou more near – than kindred, friend, man, wife,
Male to the female, soul to body; life
To quick action, or the warm, soft side   5
Of the resigning, yet resisting, bride.
The kiss of virgins, first-fruits of the bed,
Soft speech, smooth touch, the lips, the maidenhead –
These, and a thousand sweets, could ne'er be
So near, or dear, as thou wast once to me.   10
O thou drink of the gods and angels! – wine
That scatterest spirits and lust, whose purest shine
More radiant than the summer sunbeam shows;
Each way illustrious, brave, and like to those
Comets we see by night, whose shagged portents   15
Foretell the coming of some dire events;
Or some full flame, which with a pride aspires,
Throwing about his wild and active fires.
'Tis thou, above nectar, O divinest soul
(Eternal in thyself) that canst control   20
That which subverts whole nature – grief and care;
Vexation of the mind; and damned despair.
'Tis thou alone who, with thy mystic fan,
Workest more than wisdom, art, or nature can
To rouse the sacred madness, and awake   25
The frost-bound blood and spirits, and to make
Them frantic with thy raptures, flashing through
The soul like lightning, and as active, too.
'Tis not Apollo can, or thrice those three
Castalian sisters, sing, if wanting thee.   30
Horace, Anacreon, both lost their fame
Hadst thou not filled them with thy fire and flame.
Phoebean splendour! And thou, Thespian spring,
Of which sweet swans must drink before they sing
Their true-paced numbers and their holy lays,   35
Which makes them worthy cedar and the bays!
But why – why longer do I gaze upon

Thee with an eye of admiration,
Since I must leave thee, and, enforced, must say
To all thy witching beauties, go away?   40
But if thy whimpering looks do ask me why,
Then know, that Nature bids thee go, not I.
'Tis her erroneous self has made a brain
Uncapable of such a sovereign
As is thy powerful self. Prithee not smile: 45
Or smile more inly, lest thy looks beguile
My vows denounced in zeal, which thus much show thee:
That I have sworn but by thy looks to know thee.
Let others drink thee freely, and desire
Thee and their lips espoused, while I admire   50
And love thee – but not taste thee. Let my Muse
Fail of thy former helps, and only use
Her inadulterate strength: what's done by me
Hereafter shall smell of the lamp, not thee.

H142   **The Vision**

the dejected poet is sitting by
a brook when he has an encounter
with Diana

Sitting alone, as one forsook,
Close by a silver-shedding brook,
With hands held up to Love, I wept
And, after sorrows spent, I slept.
Then, in a vision, I did see   5
A glorious form appear to me:
A virgin's face she had; her dress
Was like a spritely Spartaness.
A silver bow with green silk strung
Down from her comely shoulders hung;   10
And, as she stood, the wanton air
Dandled the ringlets of her hair.
Her legs were such Diana shows
When, tucked up, she hunting goes
With buskins shortened to descry   15

The happy dawning of her thigh.
Which, when I saw, I made access ⌉
To kiss that tempting nakedness – ⌋
But she forbade me with a wand
Of myrtle she had in her hand   20
And, chiding me, said: 'Hence remove,
Herrick; thou art too coarse to love.'

H178   ## Corinna's Going a-Maying

Get up, get up, for shame; the blooming morn
Upon her wings presents the god unshorn.
  See how Aurora throws her fair
  Fresh-quilted colours through the air:
  Get up, sweet slug-a-bed, and see   5
  The dew-bespangling herb and tree.
Each flower has wept, and bowed toward the east
Above an hour since, yet you not dressed –
  Nay, not so much out of bed?
  When all the birds have matins said,   10
  And sung their thankful hymns? 'Tis sin –
  Nay, profanation – to keep in
Whenas a thousand virgins on this day
Spring, sooner than the lark, to fetch in May.

Rise, and put on your foliage, and be seen   15
To come forth, like the springtime, fresh, and green,
  And sweet as Flora. Take no care
  For jewels for your gown or hair –
  Fear not: the leaves will strew
  Gems in abundance upon you.   20
Besides, the childhood of the day has kept,
Against you, some orient pearls unwept.
  Come and receive them while the light
  Hangs on the dew locks of the night,
  And Titan on the eastern hill   25
  Retires himself, or else stands still

Till you come forth. Wash, dress, be brief in praying:
Few beads are best when once we go a-maying.

Come, my Corinna, come; and, coming, mark
How each field turns a street; each street a park   30
      Made green and trimmed with trees. See how
      Devotion gives each house a bough
      Or branch: each porch, each door, ere this
      An ark, a tabernacle is,
Made up of whitethorn neatly interwove,   35
As if here were those cooler shades of love.
      Can such delights be in the street
      And open fields, and we not see it?
      Come, we'll abroad, and let's obey
      The proclamation made for May,   40
And sin no more, as we have done, by staying,
But, my Corinna, come, let's go a-maying.

There's not a budding boy or girl this day
But is got up and gone to bring in May.
      A deal of youth, ere this, is come   45
      Back, and with whitethorn laden home.
      Some have dispatched their cakes and cream
      Before that we have left to dream;
And some have wept, and wooed, and plighted troth,
And chose their priest ere we can cast off sloth.   50
      Many a green gown has been given;
      Many a kiss, both odd and even;
      Many a glance, too, has been sent
      From out the eye, love's firmament;
Many a jest told of the key's betraying   55
This night, and locks picked – yet we're not a-maying.

Come, let us go while we are in our prime,
And take the harmless folly of the time.
      We shall grow old apace, and die
      Before we know our liberty.   60
      Our life is short, and our days run
      As fast away as does the sun,
And, as a vapour or a drop of rain,

Once lost can ne'er be found again:
  So when or you or I are made   65
  A fable song, or fleeting shade,
  All love, all liking, all delight
Lies drowned with us in endless night.
Then, when time serves, and we are but decaying,
Come, my Corinna, come: let's go a-maying.   70

  # Upon a Child: An Epitaph

  But born and, like a short delight,
  I glided past my parents' sight.
  That done, the harder Fates denied
  My longer stay, and so I died.
  If, pitying my sad parents' tears,   5
  You'll spill a tear or two with theirs,
  And with some flowers my grave bestrew,
  Love and they'll thank you for it. Adieu.

  # To His Dying Brother,
  # Master William Herrick

Life of my life, take not so soon thy flight,
But stay the time till we have bade goodnight.
Thou hast both wind and tide with thee: thy way
As soon dispatched is by the night as day.
Let us not, then, so rudely henceforth go   5
Till we have wept, kissed, sighed, shook hands, or so.
There's pain in parting, and a kind of hell
When once true lovers take their last farewell.
What? Shall we two our endless leaves take here

Without a sad look, or a solemn tear?   10
He knows not love that hath not this truth proved:
Love is most loath to leave the thing beloved.
Pay we our vows, and go. Yet, when we part,
Then, even then, I will bequeath my heart
Into thy loving hands, for I'll keep none   15
To warm my breast when thou, my pulse, art gone.
No, here I'll last, and walk (a harmless shade)
About this urn wherein thy dust is laid,
To guard it so as nothing here shall be
Heavy to hurt those sacred seeds of thee.   20

H187   **The Olive Branch**

Sadly I walked within the field
To see what comforts it would yield;
And as I went my private way,
An olive branch before me lay,
And seeing it, I made a stay,   5
And took it up, and viewed it. Then,
Kissing the omen, said 'Amen;
Be, be it so, and let this be
A divination unto me
That, in short time, my woes shall cease,   10
And Love shall crown my end with peace.'

H193   **The Lily in a Crystal**

You have beheld a smiling rose   a
        When virgins' hands have drawn   b
        O'er it a cobweb lawn: b
And here, you see, this lily shows,   a

   Tombed in a crystal stone, c   5
More fair in this transparent case d
   Than when it grew alone, c
   And had but single grace. d

You see how cream but naked is,
   Nor dances in the eye   10
   Without a strawberry,
Or some fine tincture like to this,
   Which draws the sight thereto
More by that wantoning with it,
   Than when the paler hew   15
   No mixture did admit.

You see how amber through the streams
   More gently strokes the sight
   With some concealed delight
Than when he darts his radiant beams 20
   Into the boundless air,
Where either too much light his worth
   Doth all at once impair,
   Or set it little forth.

Put purple grapes or cherries in-   25
   To glass, and they will send
   More beauty to commend
Them, from that clean and subtle skin
   Than if they naked stood,
And had no other pride at all   30
   But their own flesh and blood,
   And tinctures natural.

Thus lily, rose, grape, cherry, cream,
   And strawberry, do stir
   More love when they transfer 35
A weak, a soft, a broken beam
   Than if they should discover
At full their proper excellence,
   Without some scene cast over
   To juggle with the sense.   40

Thus let this crystalled lily be
   A rule how far to teach

Your nakedness must reach;
And that, no further than we see
Those glaring colours laid   45
By art's wise hand, but to this end,
They should obey a shade,
Lest they too far extend.

So, though you're white as swan, or snow,
And have the power to move   50
A world of men to love:
Yet, when your lawns and silks shall flow,
And that white cloud divide
Into a doubtful twilight, then,
Then will your hidden pride   55
Raise greater fires in men.

H197   ## The Welcome to Sack

So soft streams meet; so springs with gladder smiles
Meet after long divorcement by the isles
When Love (the child of likeness) urgeth on
Their crystal natures to an union;
So meet stolen kisses when the moony nights   5
Call forth fierce lovers to their wished delights;
So kings and queens meet, when desire convinces
All thoughts but such as aim at getting princes,
As I meet thee, soul of my life and fame,
Eternal lamp of love, whose radiant flame   10
Outglares the heaven's Osiris, and thy gleams
Outshine the splendour of his midday beams!
Welcome, O welcome, my illustrious spouse:
Welcome as are the ends unto my vows.
Ay, far more welcome than the happy soil   15
The sea-scourged merchant, after all his toil,
Salutes with tears of joy when fires betray
The smoky chimneys of his Ithaca.

Where hast thou been so long from my embraces,
Poor, pitied exile? Tell me, did thy Graces   20
Fly discontented hence, and for a time
Did rather choose to bless another clime?
Or wentest thou to this end the more to move me,
By thy short absence, to desire and love thee?
Why frowns my sweet? Why won't my saint confer   25
Favours on me, her fierce idolater?
Why are those looks – those looks which have been,
Time past, so fragrant – sickly now drawn in
Like a dull twilight? Tell me, and the fault
I'll expiate with sulphur, hair, and salt;   30
And with the crystal humour of the spring
Purge hence the guilt, and kill this quarrelling.
Would thou not smile, or tell me what's amiss?
Have I been cold to hug thee, too remiss,
Too temperate in embracing? Tell me, has desire   35
To theeward died in the embers, and no fire
Left in this raked-up ash heap as a mark
To testify the glowing of a spark?
Have I divorced thee only to combine
In hot adultery with another wine?   40
True, I confess I left thee, and appeal
'Twas done by me more to confirm my zeal,
And double my affection on thee, as do those
Whose love grows more inflamed by being foes.
But to forsake thee ever, could there be   45
A thought of suchlike possibility,
When thou thyself darest say, thy isles shall lack
Grapes before Herrick leaves Canary sack?
Thou makest me airy, active to be borne,
Like Iphiclus, upon the tops of corn.   50
Thou makest me nimble, as the winged Hours,
To dance and caper on the heads of flowers,
And ride the sunbeams. Can there be a thing
Under the heavenly Isis that can bring
More love unto my life, or can present   55
My genius with a fuller blandishment?
Illustrious idol! Could the Egyptians seek
Help from the garlic, onion, and the leek,

And pay no vows to thee, who wast their best
God, and far more transcendent than the rest?   60
Had Cassius, that weak water-drinker, known
Thee in thy vine, or had but tasted one
Small chalice of thy frantic liquor, he,
As the wise Cato, had approved of thee.
Had not Jove's son, that brave Tirynthian swain,   65
Invited to the Thespian banquet, ta'en
Full goblets of thy generous blood, his sprite
Ne'er had kept heat for fifty maids that night.
Come, come and kiss me: love and lust commends
Thee and thy beauties: kiss, we will be friends   70
Too strong for Fate to break us. Look upon
Me with that full pride of complexion
As queens meet queens; or come thou to me
As Cleopatra came to Anthony,
When her high carriage did at once present   75
To the triumvir love and wonderment.
Swell up my nerves with spirit; let my blood
Run through my veins like to a hasty flood.
Fill each part full of fire, active to do
What thy commanding soul shall put it to.   80
And, till I turn apostate to thy love
(Which here I vow to serve), do not remove
Thy fires from me; but Apollo's curse
Blast these like actions, or a thing that's worse,
When these circumstant shall but live to see   85
The time that I prevaricate from thee.
Call me 'the son of beer', and then confine
Me to the tap, the toast, the turf:
Let wine ne'er shine upon me; may my numbers all
Run to a sudden death and funeral;   90
And last, when thee (dear spouse) I disavow,
Ne'er may prophetic Daphne crown my brow.

H200
Upon Gubbs. Epigram

Gubbs called his children 'kitlings,' and would bound
(Some say) for joy to see those kitlings drowned.

H202
Fair Days; Or, Dawn's Deceitful

Fair was the dawn; and but e'en now the skies
Showed like to cream inspired with strawberries.
But, on a sudden, all was changed and gone
That smiled in that first-sweet complexion.
Then thunderclaps and lightning did conspire   5
To tear the world, or set it all on fire.
What trust to things below whenas we see,
As men, the heavens have their hypocrisy?

H208
To the Virgins, to Make
Much of Time

1
Gather ye rosebuds while ye may,
    Old Time is still a-flying,
And this same flower that smiles today
    Tomorrow will be dying.

2
The glorious lamp of heaven, the sun,   5
    The higher he's a-getting,

The sooner will his race be run,
    And nearer he's to setting.

3

That age is best which is the first,
    When youth and blood are warmer;   10
But, being spent, the worse and worst
    Times still succeed the former.

4

Then be not coy, but use your time,
    And, while ye may, go marry;
For, having lost but once your prime,   15
    You may for ever tarry.

H210

To His Friend, on the Untuneable Times

Play I could once; but (gentle friend) you see
My harp hung up, here on the willow tree.
Sing I could, once, and bravely, too, inspire
(With luscious numbers) my melodious lyre.
Draw I could, once (although not stocks or stones,   5
Amphion-like), men made of flesh and bones,
Whether I would. But (ah!) I know not how,
I feel in me this transmutation now.
Grief, my dear friend, has first my harp unstrung,
Withered my hand, and palsy-struck my tongue.   10

H213
A Pastoral Upon the Birth
of Prince Charles,
Presented to the King
and Set by Master Nicholas Lanier

The speakers: Myrtillo, Amyntas, and Amaryllis

AMYNT: Good day, Myrtillo.

MYRT: And to you no less;
And all fair signs lead on our shepherdess.

AMAR: With all white luck to you.

MYRT: But say, what news
Stirs in our sheep-walk?

AMYNT: None, save that my ewes
My wethers, lambs, and wanton kids are well,   5
Smooth, fair, and fat – none better can I tell;
Or that this day Menalcas keeps a feast
For his sheep-shearers.

MYRT: True, these are the least.
But, dear Amyntas, and sweet Amaryllis,
Rest but a while here by this bank of lilies,   10
And lend a gentle ear to one report
The country has.

AMYNT: From whence?

AMAR: From whence?

MYRT: The court.

Three days before the shutting-in of May
(With whitest wool be ever crowned that day!),
To all our joy a sweet-faced child was born,   15
More tender than the childhood of the morn.

CHORUS: Pan pipe to him, and bleats of lambs and sheep
Let lullaby the pretty prince asleep!

MYRT: And that his birth should be more singular,
At noon of day was seen a silver star,   20
Bright as the wise men's torch which guided them
To God's sweet babe when born at Bethlehem;
When golden angels (some have told me)

Sung out at his birth with heavenly minstrelsy.
AMYNT: O rare! But is it a trespass if we three   25
Should wend along his babyship to see?
MYRT: Not so, not so.
CHORUS: But if it chance to prove
At most a fault, 'tis but a fault of love.
AMAR: But, dear Myrtillo, I have heard it told
Those learned men brought incense, myrrh, and
    gold   30
From countries far, with store of spices sweet,
And laid them down for offerings at his feet.
MYRT: 'Tis true, indeed; and each of us will bring
Unto our smiling, and our blooming, king,
A neat, though not so great, an offering.   35
AMAR: A garland for my gift shall be
Of flowers ne'er sucked by the thieving bee,
And all most sweet – yet all less sweet than he.
AMYNT: And I will bear along with you
Leaves dropping down the honeyed dew,   40
With oaten pipes as sweet as new.
MYRT: And I a sheephook will bestow,
To have his little kingship know,
As he's a prince, he's a shepherd, too.
CHORUS: Come, let's away, and quickly let's be dressed,   45
And quickly give: the swiftest grace is best.
And when before him we have laid our treasures,
We'll bless the babe, then back to country pleasures.

H227   # To Music, to Becalm His Fever

1

Charm me asleep, and melt me so
    With thy delicious numbers
That, being ravished, hence I go
    Away in easy slumbers.

Ease my sick head,   5
And make my bed,
Thou power that canst sever
From me this ill,
And quickly still
(Though thou canst not kill)   10
My fever.

2

Thou sweetly canst convert the same
From a consuming fire
Into a gentle-licking flame,
And make it thus expire.   15
Then make me weep
My pains alseep,
And give me such reposes
That I – poor I –
May think thereby   20
I live and die
'Mongst roses.

3

Fall on me like a silent dew,
Or like those maiden showers
Which, by the peep of day, do strew
A baptism o'er the flowers.   25
Melt, melt my pains
With thy soft strains
That, having ease me given,
With full delight   30
I leave this light,
And take my flight
For heaven.

H238

To the Rose. Song

1

Go, happy rose and, interwove
With other flowers, bind my love.
    Tell her, too, she must not be
    Longer flowing, linger free,
    That so oft has fettered me.   5

2

Say, if she's fretful, I have bands
Of pearl, of gold, to bind her hands:
    Tell her, if she struggle still,
    I have myrtle rods (at will)
    For to tame, though not to kill.   10

3

Take thou my blessing thus, and go,
And tell her this – but do not so,
    Lest a handsome anger fly
    Like a lightning from her eye,
    And burn thee up as well as I.   15

H250

The Hock-Cart; Or, Harvest Home
To the Right Honourable Mildmay,
Earl of Westmorland

Come, sons of summer, by whose toil
We are the lords of wine and oil;
By whose tough labours, and rough hands,
We rip up first, then reap our lands.
Crowned with the ears of corn, now come,   5
And to the pipe sing harvest home.
Come forth, my lord, and see the cart
Dressed up with all the country art.

See, here a malkin, there a sheet,
As spotless pure as it is sweet: 10
The horses, mares, and frisking fillies
Clad, all, in linen, white as lilies.
The harvest swains, and wenches, bound
All for joy to see the hock-cart crowned.
About the cart, hear how the rout   15
Of rural younglings raise the shout,
Pressing before, some coming after –
Those with a shout, and these with laughter.
Some bless the cart; some kiss the sheaves;
Some prank them up with oaken leaves; 20
Some cross the fill-horse; some with great
Devotion stroke the home-borne wheat,
While other rustics, less attent
To prayers than to merriment
Run after with their breeches rent.   25
Well, on, brave boys, to your lord's hearth,
Glittering with fire, where, for your mirth,
Ye shall see first the large and chief
Foundation of your feast, fat beef,
With upper stories, mutton, veal   30
And bacon (which makes full the meal),
With several dishes standing by,
As – here a custard, there a pie,
And here all-tempting frumenty.
And for to make the merry cheer   35
(If smirking wine be wanting here),
There's that which drowns all care – stout beer;
Which freely drink to your lord's health,
Then to the plough, the commonwealth;
Next to your flails, your fans, your vats; 40
Then to the maids with wheaten hats.
To the rough sickle and crooked scythe,
Drink, frolic boys, till all be blithe.
Feed and grow fat, and, as ye eat,
Be mindful that the labouring neat   45
(As you) may have their fill of meat.
And know, besides, ye must revoke
The patient ox unto the yoke,

And all go back unto the plough
And harrow (though they're hanged up now).   50
And, you must know, your lord's word's true –
Feed him ye must, whose food fills you;
And that this pleasure is like rain,   ends on a triple rhyme
Not sent ye for to drown your pain,
But for to make it spring again.   55

H254   ## To Music: A Song

Music, thou queen of heaven, care-charming spell,
That strikes a stillness into hell:
Thou tamest tigers, and fierce storms that rise,
With thy soul-melting lullabies.
Fall down, down, down, from those thy chiming spheres   5
To charm our souls as thou enchantest our ears.

H257   ## To Primroses Filled
with Morning Dew

1
Why do ye weep, sweet babes? Can tears
        Speak grief in you
        Who were but born
    Just as the modest morn
    Teemed her refreshing dew?   5
Alas, you have not known that shower
        That mars a flower;
        Nor felt the unkind
    Breath of a blasting wind.
    Nor are ye worn with years,   10

Or warped, as we,
     Who think it strange to see
Such pretty flowers (like to orphans young)
To speak by tears before ye have a tongue.

2

Speak, whimpering younglings, and make known   15
          The reason why
          Ye droop and weep.
     Is it for want of sleep,
     Or childish lullaby?
Or that ye have not seen as yet   20
          The violet,
          Or brought a kiss
     From that sweetheart to this?
     No, no, this sorrow shown
          By your tears shed,   25
     Would have this lecture read:
That things of greatest, so of meanest worth,
Conceived with grief are, and with tears brought forth.

H258   **How Roses Came Red**

1

Roses at first were white,
     Till they could not agree
Whether my Sappho's breast
     Or they more white should be.

2

But, being vanquished quite,   5
     A blush their cheeks bespread;
Since which (believe the rest)
     The roses first came red.

H264

To the King

If, when these lyrics, Caesar, you shall hear,
And that Apollo shall so touch your ear
As for to make this, that, or any one
Number, your own by free adoption,
That verse of all the verses here shall be   5
The heir to this great realm of poetry.

H274

To Meadows

1

Ye have been fresh and green,
   Ye have been filled with flowers;
And ye the walks have been
   Where maids have spent their hours.

2

You have beheld how they   5
   With wicker arks did come
To kiss, and bear away
   The richer cowslips home.

3

You've heard them sweetly sing,
   And seen them in a round: 10
Each virgin, like a spring,
   With honeysuckles crowned.

4

But now we see none here
   Whose silvery feet did tread,
And with dishevelled hair   15
   Adorned this smoother mead.

5
Like unthrifts, having spent
    Your stock, and needy grown,
You're left here to lament
    Your poor estates, alone.   20

Oberon's Feast

Shapcott, to thee the fairy state
I, with discretion, dedicate,
Because thou prizest things that are
Curious and unfamiliar.
Take first the feast – these dishes gone,   5
We'll see the fairy court anon.

A little mushroom table spread,
After short prayers they set on bread:
A moon-parched grain of purest wheat,
With some small glittering grit, to eat   10
His choice bits with. Then, in a trice,
They make a feast less great than nice.
But all this while his eye is served,
We must not think his ear was starved,
But that there was in place, to stir   15
His spleen, the chirring grasshopper,
The merry cricket, puling fly,
The piping gnat, for minstrelsy.
And now, we must imagine first
The elves present, to quench his thirst,   20
A pure seed-pearl of infant dew,
Brought and besweetened in a blue
And pregnant violet; which done,
His kitling eyes begin to run
Quite through the table, where he spies   25

The horns of paper butterflies,
Of which he eats, and tastes a little
Of what we call the cuckoo's spittle.
A little fuzzball pudding stands
By, yet not blessed by his hands,   30
That was too coarse. But then forthwith
He ventures boldly on the pith
Of sugared rush, and eats the sag
And well-bestrutted bee's sweet bag,
Gladding his palate with some store   35
Of emmet's eggs: what would he more,
But beards of mice, a newt's stewed thigh,
A bloated earwig, and a fly;
With the red-capped worm that's shut
Within the concave of a nut,   40
Brown as his tooth? A little moth,
Late fattened in a piece of cloth;
With withered cherries, mandrakes' ears,
Moles' eyes: to these the slain-stag's tears,
The unctuous dewlaps of a snail,   45
The broken heart of nightingale
O'ercome in music; with a wine
Ne'er ravished from the flattering vine,
But gently pressed from the soft side
Of the most sweet and dainty bride,   50
Brought in a dainty daisy, which
He fully quaffs up to bewitch
His blood to height; this done, commended
Grace by his priest, the feast is ended.

H306   # On Himself

Here down my wearied limbs I'll lay;
My pilgrim's staff, my weed of grey,
My palmer's hat, my scallop's shell,
My cross, my cord, and all – farewell.

For having now my journey done   5
(Just at the setting of the sun),
Here I have found a chamber fit –
God and good friends be thanked for it –
Where, if I can a lodger be
A little while from tramplers free,   10
At my uprising next I shall,
If not requite, yet thank ye all.
Meanwhile, the holy rood hence fright
The fouler fiend and evil sprite,
From scaring you or yours this night.   15

H316

To Daffodils

1

Fair daffodils, we weep to see
  You haste away so soon:
As yet the early-rising sun
  Has not attained his noon.
              Stay, stay,   5
    Until the hasting day
              Has run
    But to the evensong,
And, having prayed together, we
          Will go with you along.   10

2

We have short time to stay, as you –
  We have as short a spring;
As quick a growth to meet decay,
    As you or any thing.
              We die,   15
    As your hours do, and dry
              Away,
    Like to the summer's rain,
Or as the pearls of morning's dew,
    Ne'er to be found again.   20

H318 **Upon a Lady That Died in Childbed, and Left a Daughter behind Her**

As gillyflowers do but stay   *a*   *opens with a beautiful*
To blow, and seed, and so away;   *a*   *triple rhyme*
So you, sweet lady (sweet as May),   *a*
The garden's glory, lived awhile   *b*
To lend the world your scent and smile.   *b*   5
turns But when your own fair print was set   *c*
here Once in a virgin flosculet   *c*
(Sweet as yourself, and newly-blown),   *d*
To give that life, resigned your own: *d*
But so, as still the mother's power   *e*
Lives in the pretty lady flower.   *e*   10

H336 **His Age: Dedicated to His Peculiar Friend, Master John Weekes, Under the Name of Posthumus**

1   *the template*
⁴ Ah, Posthumus! Our years hence fly   *a*
⁴ And leave no sound; nor piety,   *a*
²   Or prayers, or vow   *b*
⁴ Can keep the wrinkle from the brow: *b*
²   But we must on,   *c*   5
⁴ As Fate does lead or draw us: none,   *c*
⁴ None, Posthumus, could e'er decline   *d*
⁴ The doom of cruel Proserpine.   *d*

2
The pleasing wife, the house, the ground,
Must all be left, no one plant found   10
To follow thee

Save only the cursed cypress tree.
                         A merry mind
Looks forward, scorns what's left behind:
Let's live, my Weekes, then, while we may,   15
And here enjoy our holiday.

                         3
We've seen the past-best times, and these
Will ne'er return. We see the seas
                         And moons to wane,
But they fill up their ebbs again: 20
                         But vanished man,
Like to a lily lost, ne'er can,
Ne'er can repullulate, or bring
His days to see a second spring.

                         4
But on we must, and thither tend   25
Where Ancus and rich Tullus blend
                         Their sacred seed:
Thus has infernal Jove decreed –
                         We must be made,
Ere long, a song, ere long, a shade.   30
Why, then, since life to us is short,
Let's make it full up by our sport.

                         5
Crown we our heads with roses, then,
And anoint with Tyrian balm; for when
                         We two are dead,   35
The world with us is buried.
                         Then live we free
As is the air, and let us be
Our own fair wind, and mark each one
Day with the white and lucky stone.   40

                         6
We are not poor, although we have
No roofs of cedar, nor our brave
                         Baiae, nor keep
Account of such a flock of sheep,
                         Nor bullocks fed   45

To lard the shambles, barbels bred
To kiss our hands. Nor do we wish
For Pollio's lampreys in our dish.

7

If we can meet, and so confer
Both by a shining salt-cellar,   50
           And have our roof
(Although not arched) yet weather-proof,
           And ceiling free
From that cheap candle-bawdry,
We'll eat our bean with that full mirth   55
As we were lords of all the earth.

8

Well, then – on what seas we are tossed,
Our comfort is, we can't be lost.
           Let the winds drive
Our bark; yet she will keep alive   60
           Amidst the deeps:
'Tis constancy, my Weekes, which keeps
The pinnace up; which, though she errs
I'the seas, she saves her passengers.

9

Say we must part (sweet mercy bless   65
Us both i'the sea, camp, wilderness):
           Can we so far
Stray to become less circular
           Than we are now?
No, no, that self-same heart, that vow   70
Which made us one, shall ne'er undo,
Or ravel so, to make us two.

10

Live in thy peace. As for myself,
When I am bruised on the shelf
           Of time, and show   75
My locks behung with frost and snow;
           When, with the rheum,
The cough, the phthisic, I consume
Unto an almost-nothing – then,
The ages fled, I'll call again,   80

11

And, with a tear, compare these last
Lame and bad times with those are past;
     While Baucis by
(My old, lean wife) shall kiss it dry.
      And so we'll sit   85
By the fire, foretelling snow and sleet
And weather by our aches, grown
Now old enough to be our own

12

True calendars, as puss's ear
Washed o'er, to tell what change is near.   90
      Then, to assuage
The gripings of the chine by age,
      I'll call my young
Iulus to sing such a song
I made upon my Julia's breast,   95
And of her blush at such a feast.

13

Then shall he read that flower of mine
Enclosed within a crystal shrine;
      A primrose next;
A piece, then, of a higher text,   100
      For to beget
In me a more transcendent heat
Than that insinuating fire
Which crept into each aged sire

14

When the fair Helen, from her eyes,   105
Shot forth her loving sorceries.
     At which I'll rear
Mine aged limbs above my chair,
      And, hearing it,
Flutter and crow, as in a fit   110
Of fresh concupiscence, and cry
'No lust there's like to poetry.'

15

Thus, frantic, crazy man (God wot)
I'll call to mind things half-forgot,

        And, oft between,   115
Repeat the times that I have seen!
           Thus, ripe with tears,
And twisting my Iulus' hairs,
Doting I'll weep and say: 'In truth,
Baucis, these were my sins of youth.'   120

16

Then, next, I'll cause my hopeful lad
(If a wild apple can be had)
         To crown the hearth
(Lar thus conspiring with our mirth),
           Then to infuse   125
Our browner ale into the cruse;
Which, sweetly spiced, we'll first carouse
Unto the Genius of the house.

17

Then the next health to friends of mine
(Loving the brave Burgundian wine),   130
          High sons of pith,
Whose fortunes I have frolicked with:
           Such as could well
Bear up the magic bough and spell,
And, dancing 'bout the mystic thyrse,   135
Give up the just applause to verse.

18

To those, and then again to thee,
We'll drink, my Weekes, until we be
         Plump as the cherry
(Though not so fresh), yet full as merry   140
           As the cricket,
The untamed heifer, or the pricket,
Until our tongues shall tell our ears
We're younger by a score of years.

19

Thus, till we see the fire less shine   145
From the embers than the kitling's eyen,
           We'll sit up,
Sphering about the wassail cup
           To all those times
Which gave me honour for my rhymes.   150
The coal once spent, we'll then to bed,
Far more than night bewearied.

H349

Her Legs

Fain would I kiss my Julia's dainty leg,
Which is as white and hairless as an egg.

H376

Upon His Kinswoman
Mistress Elizabeth Herrick

Sweet virgin, that I do not set
The pillars up of weeping jet
Or mournful marble, let thy shade
Not wrathful seem, or fright the maid
Who hither at her wonted hours   5
Shall come to strew thy earth with flowers.
No – know, blessed maid, when there's not one
Remainder left of brass or stone,
Thy living epitaph shall be,
Though lost in them, yet found in me.   10
Dear, in thy bed of roses, then –
Till this world shall dissolve as men –
Sleep, while we hide thee from the light,
Drawing thy curtains round: good night.

H389   # A Just Man

A just man's like a rock that turns the wrath
Of all the raging waves into a froth.

H390   # Upon a Hoarse Singer

Sing me to death; for, till thy voice be clear,
'Twill never please the palate of mine ear.

H441   # To Daisies, Not to Shut so Soon

1
Shut not so soon: the dull-eyed night
    Has not as yet begun
To make a seizure on the light,
    Or to seal up the sun.

2
No marigolds yet closed are;   5
    No shadows great appear;
Nor doth the early shepherds' star
    Shine like a spangle here.

3
Stay but till my Julia close
    Her life-begetting eye;   10
And let the whole world then dispose
    Itself to live or die.

Oberon's Palace

H443

After the feast (my Shapcott) see,
The fairy court I give to thee,
Where we'll present our Oberon led
Half tipsy to the fairy bed,
Where Mab he finds, who there doth lie   5
Not without mickle majesty.
Which done, and thence removed the light,
We'll wish both them and thee goodnight.

Full as a bee with thyme, and red
As cherry harvest, now high fed   10
For lust and action, on he'll go
To lie with Mab, though all say no.
Lust has no ears: he's sharp as thorn,
And fretful – carries hay in his horn,
And lightning in his eyes – and flings   15
Among the elves (if moved) the stings
Of peltish wasps. We'll know his guard:
Kings, though they're hated, will be feared.
Wine leads him on. Thus to a grove
(Sometimes devoted unto love)   20
Tinselled with twilight, he and they
Lead by the shine of snails – a way
Beat with numerous feet which, by
Many a neat perplexity,
Many a turn, and many a cross-   25
Track, they redeem a bank of moss,
Spongy and swelling, and far more
Soft than the finest Leominster ore,
Mildly disparkling, like those fires
Which break from the enjewelled tires   30
Of curious brides, or like those mites
Of candied dew in moony nights.
Upon this convex, all the flowers
Nature begets by the sun and showers
Are to a wild digestion brought,   35
As if Love's sampler here was wrought,
Or Cytherea's ceston, which

All with temptation doth bewitch.
Sweet airs move here, and more divine
Made by the breath of great-eyed kine   40
Who, as they low, impearl with milk
The four-leaved grass, or moss like silk.
The breath of monkeys, met to mix
With musk-flies, are the aromatics
Which cense this arch; and here and there,   45
And farther off, and everywhere
Throughout the brave mosaic yard
Those picks, or diamonds, in the card,
With pips of hearts, of club, and spade,
Are here most neatly interlaid.   50
Many a counter, many a die,
Half-rotten, and without an eye,
Lies hereabouts; and, for to pave
The excellency of this cave,
Squirrels' and children's teeth late shed   55
Are neatly here enchequered
With brown toadstones, and the gum
That shines upon the bluer plum.
The nails fallen off by the whitlows: Art's
Wise hand enchasing here those warts   60
Which we to others from ourselves
Sell, and brought hither by the elves.
The tempting mole, stolen from the neck
Of the shy virgin, seems to deck
The holy entrance, where within   65
The room is hung with the blue skin
Of shifted snake, enfriezed throughout
With eyes of peacocks' trains, and trout-
Flies curious wings; and, these among,
Those silver pence that cut the tongue   70
Of the red infant, neatly hung.
The glowing glow-worm's eyes; the shining scales
Of silvery fish; wheat-straws; the snail's
Soft candle-light; the kitling's eyen;
Corrupted wood, serve here for shine.   75
No glaring light of bold-faced day,
Or other over-radiant ray,

Ransacks this room, but what weak beams
Can make reflected from these gems,
And multiply: such is the light,   80
But ever doubtful, day or night.
By this quaint taperlight he winds
His errors up; and now he finds
His moon-tanned Mab as somewhat sick,
And (Love knows) tender as a chick.   85
Upon six dandelions, high-
Reared, lies her elvish majesty,
Whose woolly bubbles seemed to drown
Her Mabship in obedient down.
For either sheet was spread the caul   90
That doth the infant's face enthrall
When it is born (by some enstyled
The lucky omen of the child);
And, next to these, two blankets o'er-
Cast of the finest gossamer.   95
And then a rug of carded wool
Which, sponge-like drinking of the dull
Light of the moon, seemed to comply,
Cloud-like, the dainty deity.
Thus soft she lies and, overhead,   100
A spinner's circle is bespread
With cobweb curtains, from the roof
So neatly sunk as that no proof
Of any tackling can declare
What gives it hanging in the air.   105
The fringe about this are those threads
Broke at the loss of maidenheads,
And all behung with these pure pearls
Dropped from the eyes of ravished girls
Or writhing brides when, panting, they   110
Give unto love the straiter way.
For music now he has the cries
Of feigned-lost virginities,
The which the elves make to excite
A more unconquered appetite.   115
The king's undressed; and now, upon
The gnats' watchword, the elves are gone;

And now the bed, and Mab, possessed
Of this great-little kingly quest.
We'll nobly think, what's to be done   120
He'll do no doubt: this flax is spun.

To His Peculiar Friend,
Master Thomas Shapcott, Lawyer

I've paid thee what I promised; that's not all.
Besides, I give thee here a verse that shall
(When hence thy circum-mortal part is gone)
Archlike hold up thy name's inscription.
Brave men can't die whose candid actions are   5
Writ in the poet's endless calendar,
Whose vellum and whose volume is the sky,
And the pure stars the praising poetry.
                                        Farewell.

To Groves

Ye silent shades, whose each tree here
Some relic of a saint doth wear;
Who, for some sweetheart's sake, did prove
The fire and martyrdom of love.
Here is the legend of those saints   5
That died for love, and their complaints:
Their wounded hearts and names we find
Encarved upon the leaves and rind.
Give way, give way to me, who come
Scorched with the self-same martyrdom,   10
And have deserved as much (Love knows)

As to be canonised 'mongst those
Whose deeds and deaths here written are
Within your greeny calendar.
By all those virgin fillets hung   15
Upon your boughs, and requiems sung
For saints and souls departed hence
(Here honoured still with frankincense);
By all those tears that have been shed
As a drink-offering to the dead;   20
By all those true-love-knots that be
With mottoes carved on every tree;
By sweet Saint Phillis: pity me.
By dear Saint Iphis, and the rest
Of all those other saints now blessed –   25
Me, me, forsaken, here admit
Among your myrtles to be writ,
That my poor name may have the glory
To live remembered in your story.

H467

To Blossoms

1

Fair pledges of a fruitful tree,
     Why do ye fall so fast?
     Your date is not so past
But you may stay yet here awhile
     To blush, and gently smile,   5
                And go at last.

2

What, were ye born to be
     An hour or half's delight,
     And so to bid goodnight?
'Twas pity Nature brought ye forth   10
     Merely to show your worth,
                And lose you quite.

3
But you are lovely leaves, where we
  May read how soon things have
  Their end, though ne'er so brave;
And after they have shown their pride   15
  Like you awhile, they glide
        Into the grave.

H475   Upon His Departure Hence

Thus I
Pass by,
And die,
As one
Unknown   5
And gone:
I'm made
A shade,
And laid
I'the grave;   10
There have
My cave,
Where tell
I dwell:
Farewell.   15

H484   Upon Julia's Hair Filled With Dew

Dew sat on Julia's hair,
      And spangled, too,
Like leaves that laden are
      With trembling dew;

Or glittered to my sight,   5
    As when the beams
Have their reflected light
    Danced by the streams.

H499   # To Julia

Julia, when thy Herrick dies,
Close thou up thy poet's eyes;
And his last breath, let it be
Taken in by none but thee.

H537   # To Marigolds

Give way, and be ye ravished by the sun
(And hang the head whenas the act is done);
Spread as he spreads, wax less as he does wane,
And, as he shuts, close up to maids again.

H540   # Anacreontic

Born I was to be old,
    And for to die here;
After that, in the mould
    Long for to lie here.
But, before that day comes,   5
    Still I be boozing,
For I know that in tombs
    There's no carousing.

H575   # The Apparition of His Mistress
              ## Calling Him to Elysium

              ### Desunt nonnulla——

Come, then, and like two doves with silvery wings
Let our souls fly to the shades, where ever springs
Sit smiling in the meads; where balm and oil,
Roses and cassia, crown the untilled soil;
Where no disease reigns, or infection comes   5
To blast the air, but ambergris and gums.
This, that, and every thicket doth transpire
More sweet than storax from the hallowed fire;
Where every tree a wealthy issue bears
Of fragrant apples, blushing plums or pears;   10
And all the shrubs, with sparkling spangles, show
Like morning sunshine tinselling the dew.
Here in green meadows sits eternal May,
Purfling the margents, while perpetual day
So double-gilds the air as that no night   15
Can ever rust the enamel of the light.
Here, naked younglings, handsome striplings, run
Their goals for virgins' kisses, which, when done,
Then unto dancing forth the learned round
Commixed they meet, with endless roses crowned.   20
And here we'll sit on primrose banks, and see
Love's chorus led by Cupid; and we'll be
Two loving followers, too, unto the grove
Where poets sing the stories of our love.
There thou shalt hear divine Musaeus sing   25
Of Hero and Leander; then I'll bring
Thee to the stand where honoured Homer reads
His *Odysseys* and his high *Iliads*,
About whose throne the crowd of poets throng
To hear the incantation of his tongue.   30
To Linus, then to Pindar; and, that done,
I'll bring thee, Herrick, to Anacreon,
Quaffing his full-browed bowls of burning wine,

And in his raptures speaking lines of thine
Like to his subject; and as his frantic   35
Looks show him truly Bacchanalian-like,
Besmeared with grapes, welcome he shall ye hither,
Where both may rage, both drink and dance together.
Then stately Virgil, witty Ovid (by
Whom Corinna sits, and doth comply   40
With ivory wrists his laureate head, and steeps
His eye in dew of kisses while he sleeps).
Then soft Catullus, sharp-fanged Martial,
And towering Lucan, Horace, Juvenal,
And snaky Persius – these and those whom rage   45
(Dropped from the jars of heaven) filled to engage
All times unto their frenzies – thou shalt there
Behold them in a spacious theatre.
Among which glories, crowned with sacred bays
And flattering ivy, two recite their plays –   50
Beaumont and Fletcher – swans to whom all ears
Listen while they (like sirens in their spheres)
Sing their Evadne. And still more for thee
There yet remains to know than thou canst see
By glimmering of a fancy: do but come,   55
And there I'll show thee that capacious room
In which thy father Jonson now is placed,
As in a globe of radiant fire, and graced
To be in that orb crowned that doth include
Those prophets of the former magnitude –   60
And he one chief. But hark, I hear the cock
(The bellman of the night) proclaim the clock
Of late struck one; and now I see the prime
Of day break from the pregnant east, 'tis time
I vanish. More I had to say,   *ends on a*   65
But night determines here, away.   *tetrameter*
                                                  couplet

H604

His Prayer to Ben Jonson

When I a verse shall make,
Know I have prayed thee,
For old religion's sake,
Saint Ben to aid me.

Make the way smooth for me,   5
When I, thy Herrick,
Honouring thee on my knee,
Offer my lyric.

Candles I'll give to thee,
And a new altar;   10
And thou, Saint Ben, shalt be
Writ in my psalter.

H617

His Own Epitaph

As wearied pilgrims, once possessed
Of longed-for lodging, go to rest,
So I, now having rid my way,
Fix here my buttoned staff, and stay.
Youth (I confess) hath me misled;   5
But age hath brought me right to bed.

H619

The Nightpiece: To Julia

1

Her eyes the glow-worm lend thee,
Her shooting stars attend thee;
    And the elves also,
    Whose little eyes glow
Like the sparks of fire, befriend thee.   5

2

No will-o'the-wisp mislight thee;
Nor snake or slow-worm bite thee;
    But on, on thy way
    Not making a stay,
Since ghost there's none to affright thee.   10

3

Let not the dark thee cumber;
What though the moon does slumber?
    The stars of the night
    Will lend thee their light
Like tapers clear without number.   15

4

Then, Julia, let me woo thee,
Thus, thus, to come unto me;
    And when I shall meet
    Thy silvery feet,
My soul I'll pour into thee.   20

H642

Farewell Frost; Or,
Welcome the Spring

Fled are the frosts, and now the fields appear
Reclothed in fresh and verdant diaper.
Thawed are the snows, and now the lusty spring
Gives to each mead a neat enamelling.
The palms put forth their gems, and every tree   5
Now swaggers in her leafy gallantry,
The while the Daulian minstrel sweetly sings,
With warbling notes, her Terean sufferings.
What gentle winds perspire, as if here
Never had been the northern plunderer   10
To strip the trees and fields, to their distress,
Leaving them to a pitied nakedness.
And look how, when a frantic storm doth tear
A stubborn oak or holm (long growing there),
But lulled to calmness, then succeeds a breeze   15
That scarcely stirs the nodding leaves of trees:
So, when this war (which, tempest-like, doth spoil
Our salt, our corn, our honey, wine and oil)
Falls to a temper, and doth mildly cast
His inconsiderable frenzy off at last,   20
The gentle dove may, when these turmoils cease,
Bring in her bill once more the branch of peace.

H673

To Master Denham, on his Prospective Poem

Or looked I back unto the times hence flown,
To praise those Muses, and dislike our own?
Or did I walk those pean gardens through
To kick the flowers, and scorn their odours, too?
I might (and justly) be reputed (here)   5
One nicely mad, or peevishly severe.
But, by Apollo, as I worship wit
(Where I have cause to burn perfumes to it),
So, I confess, 'tis somewhat to do well
In our high art, although we can't excel   10
Like thee, or dare the buskins to unloose
Of thy brave, bold, and sweet Maronian Muse.
But since I'm called (rare Denham) to be gone,
Take from thy Herrick this conclusion:
'Tis dignity in others if they be   15
Crowned poets, yet live princes under thee,
The while their wreaths and purple robes do shine
Less by their own gems than those beams of thine.

H686

The Funeral Rites of the Rose

The rose was sick, and smiling died;
And (being to be sanctified)
About the bed there sighing stood
The sweet and flowery sisterhood.
Some hung the head, while some did bring   5
(To wash her) water from the spring.
Some laid her forth, while others wept,
But all a solemn fast there kept.
The holy sisters some among

The sacred dirge and trental sung.   10
But ah! what sweets smelt everywhere,
As heaven had spent all perfumes there.
At last, when prayers for the dead,
And rites, were all accomplished,
They, weeping, spread a lawny loom,   15
And closed her up as in a tomb.

H706   ## How Roses Came Red

'Tis said, as Cupid danced among
The gods, he down the nectar flung;
Which, on the white rose being shed,
Made it for ever after red.

H707   ## Kings

Men are not born kings, but are men renowned,
Chose first, confirmed next, and at last are crowned.

H713   ## His Return to London

From the dull confines of the drooping west,
To see the day spring from the pregnant east,
Ravished in spirit I come – nay, more – I fly
To thee, blessed place of my nativity!
Thus, thus with hallowed foot I touch the ground   5
With thousand blessings by thy fortune crowned.

O fruitful genius, that bestowest here
An everlasting plenty, year by year!
O place, O people, manners, framed to please
All nations, customs, kindreds, languages!　　　　10
I am a free-born Roman: suffer, then,
That I amongst you live a citizen.
London my home is, though by hard fate sent
Into a long and darksome banishment.
Yet, since called back, henceforward let me be,　　　15
O native country, repossessed by thee;
For, rather than I'll to the west return,
I'll beg of thee first here to have mine urn.
Weak I am grown, and must in short time fall;
Give thou my sacred relics burial.　　　　20

H723

The Genius of His House

exhortation

Command the roof, great genius, and from thence
Into this house pour down thy influence,
That through each room a golden pipe may run
Of living water by thy benison.
Fulfil the larders, and with strengthening bread　　　5
Be evermore these bins replenished.
Next, like a bishop consecrate my ground,
That lucky fairies here may dance their round;
And after that, lay down some silver pence
The master's charge and care to recompense.　　　10
Charm then the chambers; make the beds for ease
More than for peevish sicknesses;
Fix the foundations fast, and let the roof
Grow old with time, but yet keep weatherproof.

H779 Upon Julia's Clothes

Whenas in silks my Julia goes,
Then, then, methinks, how sweetly flows
That liquefaction of her clothes.

Next, when I cast mine eyes and see
That brave vibration each way free,   5
O how that glittering taketh me!

H784 Ceremonies for Christmas

Come, bring with a noise,
My merry, merry boys,
The Christmas log to the firing;
While my good dame, she
Bids ye all be free,   5
And drink to your heart's desiring.

With the last year's brand
Light the new block, and,
For good success in his spending,
On your psalteries play,   10
That sweet music may
Come while the log is a-tinding.

Drink now the strong beer,
Cut the white loaf here,
The while the meat is a-shredding;   15
For the rare mince pie
And the plums stand by
To fill the paste that's a-kneading.

H812

The Mean

Imparity doth ever discord bring:
The mean the music makes in everything.

H823

To the King, Upon His
Taking of Leicester

This day is yours, great Charles, and in this war
Your fate and ours alike victorious are.
In her white stole now Victory does rest
Insphered with palm on your triumphant crest.
Fortune is now your captive: other kings   5
Hold but her hands; you hold both hands and wings.

H844

To His Book

Make haste away, and let one be
A friendly patron unto thee,
Lest rapt from hence I see thee lie,
Torn for the use of pastery,
Or see thy injured leaves serve well   5
To make loose gowns for mackerel,
Or see the grocers in a trice
Make hoods of thee to serve out spice.

H863

Upon Love

Love brought me to a silent grove,
    And showed me there a tree
Where some had hanged themselves for love,
    And gave a twist to me.

The halter was of silk and gold   5
    That he reached forth unto me,
No other wise than if he would
    By dainty things undo me.

He bade me then that necklace use,
    And told me, too, he maketh   10
A glorious end by such a noose
    His death for love that taketh.

'Twas but a dream; but had I been
    There really alone,
My desperate fears in love had seen   15
    Mine execution.

H892

Ceremonies for Candlemas Eve

Down with the rosemary and bays;
    Down with the mistletoe;
Instead of holly, now upraise
    The greener box, for show.

The holly hitherto did sway: 5
    Let box now domineer
Until the dancing Easter day
    Or Easter's eve appear.

Then youthful box, which now hath grace
    Your houses to renew,   10

Grown old, surrender must his place
    Unto the crisped yew.

When yew is out, then birch comes in,
    And many flowers beside;
Both of a fresh and fragrant kin   15
    To honour Whitsuntide.

Green rushes then, and sweetest bents,
    With cooler oaken boughs,
Come in for comely ornaments
    To readorn the house.   20
Thus times do shift; each thing his turn does hold;
New things succeed as former things grow old.

H898   Julia's Churching, or Purification

Put on thy holy filletings, and so
To the temple with the sober midwife go,
Attending thus, in a most solemn wise,
By those who serve the childbed mysteries.
Burn first thine incense; next, whenas thou seest   5
The candid stole thrown o'er the pious priest,
With reverend curtsies come, and to him bring
Thy free (and not decurted) offering.
All rites well ended, with fair auspice come
(As to the breaking of a bride-cake) home,   10
Where ceremonious Hymen shall for thee
Provide a second epithalamy:
She who keeps chastely to her husband's side
Is not for one, but every, night his bride;
And, stealing still with love and fear to bed,   15
Brings him not one but many a maidenhead.

H910
Upon Ben Jonson

Here lies Jonson with the rest
Of the poets, but the best.
Reader, wouldest thou more have known?
Ask his story, not his stone.
That will speak what this can't tell   5
Of his glory. So, farewell.

H911
An Ode for Him

Ah, Ben!
Say how, or when
Shall we thy guests
Meet at those lyric feasts
Made at the Sun,   5
The Dog, the Triple Tun?
Where we such clusters had
As made us nobly wild, not mad;
And yet each verse of thine
Outdid the meat, outdid the frolic wine.   10

My Ben,
Or come again,
Or send to us
Thy wit's great overplus;
But teach us yet   15
Wisely to husband it
Lest we that talent spend
And, having once brought to an end
That precious stock, the store
Of such a wit the world should have no more. 20

H913
Blame

In battles what disasters fall,
The king he bears the blame of all.

H952
On Himself

Weep for the dead, for they have lost this light;
And weep for me, lost in an endless night.
Or mourn or make a marble verse for me,
Who writ for many. Benedicite.

H1026
Saint Distaff's Day; Or,
The Morrow After Twelfth Day

Partly work, and partly play
Ye must on Saint Distaff's day:
From the plough soon free your team;
Then come home and fodder them.
If the maids a-spinning go,   5
Burn the flax and fire the tow;
Scorch their plackets, but beware
That ye singe no maiden hair.
Bring in pails of water, then
Let the maids bewash the men.   10
Give Saint Distaff all the right,
Then bid Christmas sport goodnight.
And next morrow, everyone
To his own vocation.

H1028   # His Tears to Thamesis

I send, I send here my supremest kiss
To thee, my silvery-footed Thamesis.
No more shall I reiterate thy strand,
Whereon so many stately structures stand,
Nor in the summer evenings go   5
To bathe in thee as thousand others do.
No more shall I along thy crystal glide
In barge with boughs and rushes beautified,
With soft, smooth virgins for our chaste disport,
To Richmond, Kingston, and to Hampton Court.   10
Never again shall I with finny oar
Put from, or draw unto, the faithful shore;
And landing here, or safely landing there,
Make way to my beloved Westminster,
Or to the golden Cheapside, where the earth   15
Of Julia Herrick gave to me my birth.
May all clean nymphs and curious water dames,
With swanlike state, float up and down thy streams:
No drought upon thy wanton waters fall
To make them lean and languishing at all;   20
No ruffling winds come hither to dis-ease
Thy pure and silver-wristed naiades.
Keep up your state, ye streams; and as ye spring,
Never make sick your banks by surfeiting.
Grow young with tides, and though I see ye never,   25
Receive this vow: so fare ye well for ever.

H1124

On Himself

I'll write no more of love; but now repent
Of all those times that I in it have spent.
I'll write no more of life, but wish 'twas ended,
And that my dust was to the earth commended.

H1128

On Himself

The work is done: young men and maidens set
Upon my curls the myrtle coronét
Washed with sweet ointments. Thus at last I come
To suffer in the Muses' martyrdom,
But with this comfort: if my blood be shed,   5
The Muses will wear blacks when I am dead.

H1129

The Pillar of Fame

Fame's pillar here, at last, we set,
Outduring marble, brass, or jet;
Charmed and enchanted so
As to withstand the blow
Of o v e r t h r o w.   5
Nor shall the seas,
O r o u t r a g e s
Of storms o'erbear
What we uprear.
Though kingdoms fall,   10
This pillar never shall
Decline or waste at all;
But stand for ever by his own
Firm and well-fixed foundation.

H1130   # To His Book's End

To his book's end this last line he'd have placed:
Jocund his Muse was, but his life was chaste.

FINIS

from **His Noble Numbers;** Or, His Pious Pieces

His Prayer for Absolution

For those my unbaptised rhymes,
Writ in my wild, unhallowed times;
For every sentence, clause and word
That's not inlaid with thee, my Lord,
Forgive me, God, and blot each line   5
Out of my book that is not thine.
But if, 'mongst all, thou findest here one
Worthy thy benediction,
That one of all the rest shall be
The glory of my work and thee.   10

Mercy and Love

God hath two wings, which he doth ever move:
The one is mercy, and the next is love.
Under the first the sinners ever trust,
And with the last he still directs the just.

N28

Temptation

Those saints which God loves best
The devil tempts not least.

N38

Upon Time

        Time was upon
The wing, to fly away,
        And I called on
Him but a while to stay;
        But he'd be gone   5
For aught I could say.

        He held out then
A writing as he went,
        And asked me when
False man would be content   10
        To pay again
What God and Nature lent.

        An hourglass,
In which were sands but few,
        As he did pass,   15
He showed, and told me, too,
        Mine end near was;
And so away he flew.

N41

His Litany to the Holy Spirit

1
In the hour of my distress,
When temptations me oppress,
And when I my sins confess:
        Sweet Spirit, comfort me!

2

When I lie within my bed,   5
Sick in heart, and sick in head,
And with doubts discomforted:
   Sweet Spirit, comfort me!

3

When the house doth sigh and weep,
And the world is drowned in sleep,   10
Yet mine eyes the watch do keep:
   Sweet Spirit, comfort me!

4

When the artless doctor sees
No one hope but of his fees,
And his skill runs on the lees: 15
   Sweet Spirit, comfort me!

5

When his potion and his pill,
His, or none, or little skill
Meet for nothing but to kill:
   Sweet Spirit, comfort me!   20

6

When the passing-bell doth toll,
And the Furies in a shoal
Come to fright a parting soul:
   Sweet Spirit, comfort me!

7

When the tapers now burn blue,   25
And the comforters are few,
And that number more than true:
   Sweet Spirit, comfort me!

8

When the priest his last hath prayed,
And I nod to what is said   30
'Cause my speech is now decayed:
   Sweet Spirit, comfort me!

9

When God knows I'm tossed about
Either with despair or doubt,
Yet, before the glass be out: 35
     Sweet Spirit, comfort me!

10

When the tempter me pursueth
With the sins of all my youth,
And half damns me with untruth:
     Sweet Spirit, comfort me!   40

11

When the flames and hellish cries
Fright mine ears and fright mine eyes,
And all terrors me surprise:
     Sweet Spirit, comfort me!

12

When the Judgement is revealed,   45
And that opened which was sealed,
When to thee I have appealed:
     Sweet Spirit, comfort me!

N46   **To God**

I'll come, I'll creep (though thou dost threat)
Humbly unto thy mercy seat.
When I am there, this, then, I'll do:
Give thee a dart, and a dagger, too.
Next, when I have my faults confessed,   5
Naked I'll show a sighing breast,
Which, if that can't thy pity woo,
Then let thy justice do the rest,
     And strike it through.

N47   # A Thanksgiving to God for His House

Lord, thou hast given me a cell
    Wherein to dwell,
And little house, whose humble roof
    Is weatherproof,
Under the spars of which I lie   5
    Both soft and dry,
Where thou my chamber for to ward
    Hast set a guard
Of harmless thoughts to watch and keep
    Me while I sleep.   10
Low is my porch as is my fate,
    Both void of state;
And yet the threshold of my door
    Is worn by the poor,
Who thither come and freely get   15
    Good words, or meat.
Like as my parlour, so my hall
    And kitchen's small:
A little buttery, and therein
    A little bin,   20
Which keeps my little loaf of bread
    Unchipped, unflayed.
Some little sticks of thorn or briar
    Make me a fire,
Close by whose living coal I sit,   25
    And glow like it.
Lord, I confess, too, when I dine
    The pulse is thine,
And all those other bits that be
    There placed by thee: 30
The worts, the purslane, and the mess
    Of water-cress,
Which of thy kindness thou hast sent;
    And my content
Makes those, and my beloved beet,   35
    To be more sweet.
'Tis thou that crownest my glittering hearth

With guiltless mirth,
And givest me wassail bowls to drink,
    Spiced to the brink.   40
Lord, 'tis thy plenty-dropping hand
    That soils my land,
And givest me, for my bushel sown,
    Twice ten for one;
Thou makest my teeming hen to lay   45
    Her egg each day,
Besides my healthful ewes to bear
    Me twins each year;
The while the conduits of my kine
    Run cream for wine.   50
All these and better thou dost send
    Me, to this end:
That I should render, for my part,
    A thankful heart,
Which, fired with incense, I resign   55
    As wholly thine;
But the acceptance – that must be,
    My Christ, by thee.

N53

To Death

Thou biddest me come away,
And I'll no longer stay
Than for to shed some tears
For faults of former years,
And to repent some crimes   5
Done in the present times;
And next, to take a bit
Of bread, and wine with it;
To don my robes of love,
Fit for a place above;   10
To gird my loins about
With charity throughout;

And so to travel hence
With feet of innocence:
These done, I'll only cry   15
'God, mercy'; and so die.

N62   **God, and the King**

How am I bound to two! God, who doth give
The mind; the king, the means whereby I live.

N93   **Graces for Children**

What God gives, and what we take,
'Tis a gift for Christ his sake:
Be the meal of beans and peas,
God be thanked for all of these:
Have we flesh or have we fish,   5
All are fragments from his dish.
He his church save, and the king,
And our peace here, like a spring
Make it ever flourishing.

N95   **Another Grace for a Child**

Here a little child I stand,
Heaving up my either hand:
Cold as paddocks though they be,
Here I lift them up to thee,

For a benison to fall
On our meat and on us all. Amen.

The Star Song: A Carol to the King; Sung at Whitehall

The flourish of music; then followed the song

1

Tell us, thou clear and heavenly tongue,
Where is the babe but lately sprung?
Lies he the lily banks among?

2

Or say, if this new birth of ours
Sleeps, laid within some ark of flowers,   5
Spangled with dew light: thou canst clear
All doubts, and manifest the where.

3

Declare to us, bright star, if we shall seek
Him in the morning's blushing cheek,
Or search the bed of spices through   10
To find him out?

STAR: No, this ye need not do;
But only come and see him him rest,
A princely babe in his mother's breast.

CHOR: He's seen, he's seen: why, then, around   15
Let's kiss the sweet and holy ground,
And all rejoice that we have found
A king before conception crowned.

4

Come then, come then, and let us bring
Unto our pretty Twelfth-tide king   20
Each one his several offering.

CHOR: And when night comes, we'll give him wassailing;
             And, that his treble honours may be seen,
             We'll choose him king, and make his mother queen.

N121   **The Bellman**

Along the dark and silent night,
With my lantern and my light,
And the tinkling of my bell,
Thus I walk, and this I tell:
Death and dreadfulness call on   5
To the general session;
To whose dismal bar we there
All account must come to clear;
Scores of sins we've made here many;
Wiped out few – God knows if any.   10
Rise, ye debtors, then, and fall
To make payment, while I call.
Ponder this when I am gone;
By the clock 'tis almost one.

N128   **The White Island, or Place**
             of the Blessed

In this world (the isle of dreams),
While we sit by sorrows' streams,
Tears and terrors are our themes
           Reciting;

But when once from hence we fly,   5
More and more approaching nigh

Unto young eternity
    Uniting,

In that whiter island, where
Things are evermore sincere   10
(Candour here and lustre there
    Delighting);

There no monstrous fancies shall
Out of hell an horror call
To create, or cause at all,   15
    Affrighting.

There in calm and cooling sleep
We our eyes shall never steep,
But eternal watch shall keep,
    Attending   20

Pleasures such as shall pursue
Me immortalised, and you;
And fresh joys, as never, too,
    Have ending.

N129   # To Christ

I crawl, I creep: my Christ, I come
To thee for curing balsamum.
Thou hast – nay, more, thou art – the tree
Affording salve of sovereignty.
My mouth I'll lay unto thy wound   5
Bleeding, that no blood shall touch the ground;
For, rather than one drop shall fall
To waste, my Jesu, I'll take all.

N144
Long Life

The longer thread of life we spin,
The more occasion still to sin.

N153
Mora Sponsi: The Stay
of the Bridegroom

The time the bridegroom stays from hence
Is but the time of penitence.

N181
Tapers

Those tapers which we set upon the grave
In funeral pomp but this importance have:
That souls departed are not put out quite,
But, as they walked here in their vestures white,
So live in heaven in everlasting light.   5

N214
Christ's Action

Christ never did so great a work, but there
His human nature did in part appear;
Or ne'er so mean a piece but men might see
Therein some beams of his divinity;
So that, in all he did, there did combine   5
His human nature, and his part divine.

N217   # Sin

> Sin never slew a soul unless there went
> Along with it some tempting blandishment.

N218   ## Another

> Sin is an act so free that, if we shall
> Say 'tis not free, 'tis then no sin at all.

N219   ## Another

> Sin is the cause of death; and sin's alone
> The cause of God's predestination:
> And from God's prescience of man's sin doth flow
> Our destination to eternal woe.

N228   ## To Keep a True Lent

1

> Is this a fast – to keep
>   The larder lean
>   And clean
> From fat of veals and sheep?

2

Is it to quit the dish   5
    Of flesh, yet still
        To fill
The platter high with fish?

3

Is it to fast an hour,
    Or ragged to go,   10
        Or show
A downcast look and sour?

4

turns No: 'tis a fast to dole
    Thy sheaf of wheat,
        And meat,   15
Unto the hungry soul.

5

It is to fast from strife,
    From old debate,
        And hate;
To circumcise thy life;   20

6

To show a heart grief-rent;
    To starve thy sin,
        Not bin.
And that's to keep thy Lent.

Clothes for Continuance

N231

Those garments lasting evermore
Are works of mercy to the poor,
Which neither tetter, Time, or moth,
Shall fray that silk or fret this cloth.

N247
The Resurrection

That Christ did die, the pagan saith;
But that he rose, that's Christians' faith.

N248
Coheirs

We are coheirs with Christ; nor shall his own
Heirship be less by our adoption:
The number here of heirs shall from the state
Of his great birthright nothing derogate.

N249
The Number of Two

God hates the dual number, being known   a
The luckless number of division;   a
And when he blessed each several day   b
Whereon he did his curious operation,   a
'Tis never read there (as the Fathers say)   b   5
God blessed his work done on the second day: b
Wherefore two prayers ought not to be said,   c
Or by ourselves, or from the pulpit read.   c

N251
The Rose

Before man's fall the rose was born
(Saint Ambrose says) without the thorn;

But, for man's fault, then was the thorn
Without the fragrant rosebud born,
But ne'er the rose without the thorn.   5

N253   **Baptism**

The strength of baptism, that's within:
It saves the soul by drowning sin.

N263   **Good Friday: Rex Tragicus; Or,**
                  Christ Going to His Cross

Put off thy robe of purple, then go on
To the sad place of execution:
Thine hour is come, and the tormentor stands
Ready to pierce thy tender feet and hands.
Long before this the base, the dull, the rude,   5
The inconstant and unpurged multitude
Yawn for thy coming. Some ere this time cry:
'How he defers! How loath he is to die!'
Amongst this scum the soldier with his spear,
And that sour fellow with his vinegar,   10
His sponge, and stick, do ask why thou dost stay.
So do the scurf and bran, too. Go thy way,
Thy way, thou guiltless man, and satisfy
By thine approach each their beholding eye.
Not as a thief shalt thou ascend the mount,   15
But like a person of some high account:
The cross shall be thy stage, and thou shalt there
The spacious field have for thy theatre.
Thou art that Roscius, and that marked-out man,

That must this day act the tragedian   20
To wonder and affrightment; thou art he
Whom all the flux of nations comes to see,
Not those poor thieves that act their parts with thee
(Those act without regard when once a king
And God, as thou art, comes to suffering).   25
No, no, this scene from thee takes life and sense,
And soul and spirit, plot and excellence.
Why then, begin, great king! Ascend thy throne,
And thence proceed to act thy passion
To such a height, to such a period raised,   30
As hell and earth and heaven may stand amazed.
God and good angels guide thee, and so bless
Thee in thy several parts of bitterness
That those who see thee nailed unto the tree
May (though they scorn thee) praise and pity thee,   35
And we thy lovers, while we see thee keep
The laws of action, will both sigh and weep,
And bring our spices to embalm thee dead.
That done, we'll see thee sweetly buried.

N269

To His Saviour's Sepulchre:
His Devotion

Hail, holy and all-honoured tomb,
By no ill haunted: here I come,
With shoes put off, to tread thy room.
I'll not profane, by soil of sin,
Thy door as I do enter in,   5
For I have washed both hand and heart,
This, that, and every other part,
So that I dare, with far less fear
Than full affection, enter here.
Thus, thus I come to kiss thy stone   10
With a warm lip, and solemn one;

And, as I kiss, I'll here and there
Dress thee with a flowery diaper.
How sweet this place is, as from hence
Flowed all Panchaia's frankincense,   15
Or rich Arabia did commix
Here all her rare aromatics!
Let me live ever here, and stir
No one step from this sepulchre.
Ravished I am, and down I lie   20
Confused, in this brave ecstasy.
Here let me rest, and let me have
This for my heaven that was thy grave:
And, coveting no higher sphere,
I'll my eternity spend here.   25

N270

His Offering, With the Rest, at the Sepulchre

To join with them who here confer
Gifts to my saviour's sepulchre,
Devotion bids me hither bring
Somewhat for my thank-offering.
Lo! Thus I give a virgin flower   5
To dress my maiden saviour.

N271

His Coming to the Sepulchre

Hence they have borne my Lord: behold, the stone
Is rolled away, and my sweet saviour's gone!
Tell me, white angel, what is now become
Of him we lately sealed up in this tomb?

Is he from hence gone to the shades beneath,   5
To vanquish hell as here he conquered death?
If so, I'll thither follow without fear,
And live in hell if that my Christ stays there.

N272   **Of All the Good Things**

Of all the good things whatsoe'er we do,
God is the ARCHĒ, and the TELOS, too.

Notes

Text from *Hesperides; Or, The Works Both Humane and Divine of Robert Herrick, Esq* (London: 1648). This contains the religious poems as *His Noble Numbers; Or, His Pious Pieces*. Spelling and punctuation modernised.

Abbreviations
[H]: note, or information by Herrick himself
Met: Ovid, *Metamorphoses*

Hesperides

H1 title: *Argument*: theme. **2 July-flowers**: gillyflowers, or clove-scented pinks. **3 hock-carts**: festive wagons carrying home last of harvest; **wassails**: healths drunk in spiced ale especially on Christmas Eve and Twelfth Night; **wakes**: vigils for religious festivals or for the dead; also, fairs. **8 ambergris**: waxy whale-derived substance used in perfumes. **9 transshifting**: changing (i.e., peace to civil war, etc.). **12 Mab**: fairies' queen, midwife, and in charge of dreams (*Romeo and Juliet*, I.iv).

H2 To His Muse **5 cotes**: cottages; animal shelters. **6 meaner**: not elevated (i.e., not epic or tragedy). **7 reed**: shepherd's pipe, emblem of pastoral poetry. **10 bucolics**: pastoral poems (same as *eclogues*). **13 neat**: cattle. **16 take**: delight.

H3 To His Book **1 candour**: whiteness (of pages; of innocence). Such a valediction is common: e.g., Spenser, *Shepherds' Calendar*, 'To His Book'.

H5 Another **1 wipe**: the leaves of unsold books were often used as toilet paper: cf. Dryden, *MacFlecknoe* (1682), 101.

H8 When ... Verses Read **1 rehearse**: recite. **5 laurel**: emblem of poetry. **7 thyrs'**: thyrsus (ivy-entwined javelin [H]) dedicated to Bacchus, god of wine and inspiration of poetry. **8 orgies**: 'songs to Bacchus' [H].

9 rose: emblem of love; wisdom; and mystic silence. **10 Cato:** Cato Censorius (d. 149 BC), strict censor, embodied traditional Roman virtues.

H9 Upon Julia's Recovery 2 roses: beauty and mutability. **4 violet:** virginity and love. **5 primroses:** spring; youth; sickly girls. **12 beams:** gleams; red *coral* protects against ills.

H11 Parliament of Roses 5 state: ceremonial canopy. **6 tiffany:** transparent gauze muslin or *lawn*.

H17 Treason 2 He ... cherishing: Juvenal, *Satires*, 13.209–10.

H18 Two Things Odious 1–2 Two ... proud: Ecclesiasticus 25:2–4.

H20 Wounded Heart 1 sampler: apprentice piece of embroidery. **3 dropping:** drops of blood.

H22 To Anthea 3 corse: corpse. **4 laurel:** H8, 5n. **6 filletings:** headbands. **7 pitcher:** urn. **9 plat:** plot.

H29 Love ... is 1 circle: emblem of perfection; echoes R. Burton, *Anatomy of Melancholy*, 3.1.1.2.

H34 title: Carcanet = necklace or collar. **1 orient:** bright.

H35 His ... Julia 4 remora: sucking fish, believed to stop ships moving. **8 drink offering:** libation. **9 Mercy ... thee:** Proverbs 3:3.

H40 The Dream 3 Myrtle: emblem of Venus. **7–8 bee ... sting:** common image (sting = love's pains, the honey its pleasures). H echoes *Anacreontea* (i.e., light-hearted odes of 6th-century BC Greek poet Anacreon), 28.

H41 The Vine a blazon, or cataloguing of woman's body. **2 vine:** emblem of Bacchus and lust; parodies John 15:1 and echoes Johannes Secundus, *Basium* 2. **23 stock:** trunk, stump.

H50 To Robin Redbreast the bird traditionally covers the bodies of the unburied with leaves and flowers.

H52 To . . . Country **1 O . . . voice:** Jeremiah 22:29, on Coniah, who shall die an exile (H refers to the London of his birth).

H53 Cherry-ripe London street cry. **6 isle:** a reference to the notion of the Hesperides (cf. **N128**, *The White Island*).

H54 To His Mistresses **2 ambergris:** H1, 8n. **4 nectarel:** fragrant (**ambrosia** = the food, and **nectar** the drink of the gods). **5 perspire:** exhale.

H55 To Anthea **4 holy oak:** oak marking parish boundary; during 'beating of the bounds' ceremony the procession stopped by it for a gospel reading. **10 wanting:** lacking.

H57 Dreams **2 several:** separate.

H69 All Things . . . Die **3 lustres:** five-year periods.

H72 Upon . . . Elizabeth Herrick H's brother's widow; his housekeeper at Dean Prior, she died 11 April 1643.

H77 To the King. . . **2 genius:** guardian spirit; Charles I passed through Devon into Cornwall in the summer of 1644. **7 horrid:** barbaric (Virgil, *Aeneid*, 6.86). **11 white:** auspicious. **12 standard:** king's ensign.

H78 Upon Roses **1 lawn:** veil of fine linen. **2 ruffled:** carelessly heaped up (roses: **H8, 9**). **3 snugging:** snuggling.

H79 To the King and Queen . . . **1 ball:** cannonball; Discord's golden apple which, awarded by Paris to Venus, caused the Trojan War. **2 here:** the queen went abroad in 1644, with Charles in the west country. **7 oak:** the prophetic oak at Dodona (the oak also signifies kingship). **8 amber:** immortality. **10 C.M.:** cf. Aurelian Townshend's court masque *Albion's Triumph* (1632), where the renowned marital unity of the king and queen is symbolised by the 'twin, the Mary-Charles'.

H82 title: *Shade*: spirit; **religious:** revered. **1 lustres:** H69. 3n. There was a suspicion that Nicholas Herrick had killed himself. **3 hair . . . cut:** sign of grief. **4 justments:** due ceremonies. **8 effused:** tearful.

9 smallage: parsley (like the others, associated with death).

H83 *Delight in Disorder* 3 lawn: H78, 1n. **4 distraction:** confusion.

H89 *To Laurels* 5 laurel: H8. 5n.; also, immortality.

H104 *To Anthea* . . . 2 tiffanies: H11, 6n. **4 lawn:** H78, 1n. (i.e., dew).

H105 *To Electra* 6 ivory: Pelops, son of Tantalus, was boiled and fed to the gods to test their divinity. All abstained except Ceres, who ate his shoulder, which, when he was revived, was replaced with one of ivory. **9 cloud:** Ixion lusted after Juno, queen of heaven; Jupiter deceived him by forming a cloud in her shape.

H111 *A Lyric* . . . 5 vine: H41, 2n. **8 thyrs':** H8 (where also is the laurel (*bays*) of poetic inspiration). **13 Wilson and Gualtier:** Dr John **Wilson** (d. 1674), Oxford Professor of Music; James **Gualtier**, lutenist.

H115 *The Frozen Zone* . . . 3 treasures: Job 38:22. **11 zone:** climatic belt; girdle of virginity. **16 starve:** kill with cold.

H128 *Farewell to Sack*: sack = dry white wine imported from Spain and Canaries. **14 brave:** splendid. **15 shagged:** hairy. **23 fan:** winnowing basket dedicated to Bacchus (Virgil, *Georgics*, 1.166). **29 Apollo:** (Phoebus), sun god of poetry and leader of the nine Muses; the spring **Castalius** was at the foot of Mount Parnassus. **33 Thespian:** Thespis founded Greek tragedy. **36 cedar:** immortality; **bays:** H89, 5n., **111**, 8n. **44 sovereign:** king; potent cordial. **48 but:** only. **53 inadulterate:** unadulterated.

H142 *The Vision* 6 form: echoes Virgil, *Aeneid*, 1.314ff., Venus appearing to Aeneas disguised as a nymph of the virginal huntress, Diana (the combination signified chaste love). **15 buskins:** thigh boots; **descry:** disclose. **20 myrtle:** H40, 3n.

H178 *Corinna's* . . . *a-Maying* celebrates the May Day fertility festival when the young went into the woodland for sexual fun and to gather hawthorn (**may** or **whitethorn**) branches. It corresponded to the Roman festival of **Flora**, the flower goddess (late April–early May). For **Corinna**, see **H575**, 40n. **2 god unshorn:** the sun with all his rays. **3 Aurora:** dawn goddess. **20 Gems:** also, buds. **22 Against:** in expectation of; **orient:** bright. **25 Titan:** the sun. **28 beads:** prayers. **34 tabernacle:** booth (Leviticus 23:40–42). **40 proclamation:** Charles I's 'declaration . . . concerning lawful sports', 1633. **51 green:** grass-stained. **68 endless night:** Catullus, 5.

H180 *Upon a Child* . . . 3 harder: too hard.

H187 *The Olive Branch* the *olive* symbolises peace.

H193 *The Lily* . . . 1 rose: H78. **4 lily:** virginity; **crystal:** purity. **30 pride:** splendour. **37 discover:** reveal. **38 proper:** individual. **39 scene:** veil.

H197 *Welcome to Sack* cf. **H128**. **1 gladder:** most glad. **7 convinces:** vanquishes. **8 getting:** begetting. **11 Osiris:** 'the sun' [H]; i.e., the Egyptian sun god, identified also with Bacchus, god of wine. **18 Ithaca:** to which Odysseus returned after his long absence (Homer's *Odyssey*). **20 Graces:** the three daughters of Jupiter and companies of Venus, Aglaia (Beauty), Thalia (Abundance), Euphrosyne (Mirth); known as the Charites (Thanks). **30 sulphur . . . salt:** in ancient Rome, salt was sprinkled as a first offering on the sacrificial beast, and some of its head hair was thrown into the fire; **sulphur** was used to purify in sickness. **31 humour:** liquid. **40 adultery:** also, corrupt by adding inferior wine. **50 Iphiclus:** known for his fleet-footedness. **51 Hours:** daughters of the Egyptian sun god under the name of Horus; open the gates of the day and control the seasons. **54 Isis:** 'the moon' [H]; Egyptian moon goddess, wife of Osiris. **56 genius:** guardian spirit; appetite. **58 garlic . . . leek:** Numbers 11:5. **61 Cassius:** plotted the death of Caesar; reputed to drink only water. **64 Cato:** H8, 10n.; wrote a work on rural economy, *De re rustica* (*Concerning rural matters*). **65 Jove's son:** 'Hercules' [H] of Tiryns who, as a reward for delivering Thespiae from a ravaging lion, was permitted to sleep with the king's 50 daughters. **76 triumvir:** Antony ruled Rome with Lepidus and Octavian from 43 BC. **83 Apollo's curse:** Apollo = god of poetry. **85 circumstants:** bystanders. **86 prevaricate:** deviate. **88 toast:** fragments of which were floated in beer. **89 numbers:** verse. **92 Daphne:** lustfully pursued by Apollo, she was turned into a laurel, emblem of poetry: *Met.*, 1.452ff.

H208 To the Virgins . . . **1 rosebuds: H9**, 2n. **15 prime:** youth; spring.

H210 To His Friend . . . **2 harp . . . tree:** Psalm 137:2 (weeping when recalling Zion; can we sing in a strange land); *willow* = melancholy. **6 Amphion:** his harp playing had the power to move stones to build the walls of Thebes.

H213 A Pastoral . . . **Lanier:** master of the King's Music (d. 1666). The future Charles II was born 29 May 1630. **3 white luck: H77**, 11n. **17 Pan:** god of nature and shepherds. **20 star:** attested to by many (including Dryden, *Astraea Redux*, 288–9), it was a midday appearance of Hesperus. **31 store:** abundance.

H238 To the Rose . . . **1 rose: H8**, 9n. **9**, 2n. **9 myrtle: H40**, 3n.

H250 The Hock-Cart . . . see **H1**, 3n.; **Mildmay:** Mildmay Fane, 2nd earl, d. 1666. Cf. Tibullus, 2.1 on Roman corn festivals. **9 malkin:** mop; scarecrow. **21 cross:** bless; sit astride; **fill-horse:** shaft-horse. **40 fans: H128**, 23n. **45 neat:** cowherd. **47 revoke:** recall.

H254 To Music . . . **5 chiming spheres:** the sphere of each planetary orbit, guided by a daemon, was thought to emit a musical note.

H257 To Primroses . . . **H9**, 5n. **5 teemed:** brought forth.

H293 Oberon's Feast cf. *The Fairy Temple* (**H223**; not in this anthology) and **H443**. **Oberon:** the fairy king. **1 Shapcott:** Thomas, lawyer, H's friend (d. 1670). **10 grit:** coarse oatmeal. **12 nice:** minute; elegant. **16 spleen:** melancholy. **23 pregnant:** full (of dew). **24 kitling:** tiny; bright (like kitten's). **29 fuzzball:** puffball. **33 sag:** hanging; **bestrutted:** swollen. **50 bride:** bride-wort (meadow-sweet).

H306 On Himself cf. Ralegh, 'The Passionate Man's Pilgrimage'. **2 weed:** robe. **3 palmer's hat:** palmers were pilgrims to the Holy Land, from which they brought back a palm leaf; **scallop's shell:** sign that a pilgrim had visited the shrine of St James of Compostella.

H318 Upon a Lady **1 gillyflowers: H1**, 2n. **2 blow:** flower. **7 flosculet:** little flower.

H336 title: *Peculiar*:   particular; **John Weekes:** fellow priest and friend of H, they were ordained together; **Posthumus:** Roman name from Horace, *Odes*, 2.14 (the opening of which H proceeds to translate). **8 Proserpine:** abducted to hell by Hades, she became his queen (**doom** = sentence; here, of death). **23 repullulate:** bud again. **26 Ancus, Tullus:** 4th and 3rd Roman kings. **34 Tyrian balm:** sweet wine (**roses:** Wisdom of Solomon 2:8). **43 Baiae:** sea resort. **46 shambles:** meat-market; **barbels:** kind of carp. **48 Pollio:** had a slave flung into a pool to be eaten by **lampreys. 54 candle-bawdry:** dirt from candles. **68 circular:** perfectly united. **92 chine:** back. **94 Iulus:** i.e., son. **97 flower of mine:** H193; **primrose:** H257. **105 Helen:** of Troy. **122 wild apple:** log. **124 Lar:** household god. **126 cruse:** pot. **131 pith:** strength. **135 thyrse:** H8, 7n. **142 pricket:** young stag. **148 wassail cup:** H1, 3n.

H376 title: *Elizabeth Herrick*:   (1609–30), daughter of brother William. **8 brass, stone:** Horace, *Odes*, 3.30.

H441 *To Daisies* . . . 7 shepherds' star: Hesperus, the evening star.

H443 *Oberon's Palace* 1 H293, 1n. **5 Mab:** H1, 12n. **6 mickle:** much. **14 horn:** hay was used to cover the horns of an angry ox. **17 peltish:** angry. **26 redeem:** reach. **28 Leominster ore:** Herefordshire wool. **31 brides:** the head-dresses of elegant brides. **36 sampler:** H20, 1n. **37 ceston:** Venus's girdle, made by Vulcan, caused people to fall in love with her. **48 pick:** diamond; **pip:** spot (on playing cards). **57 toadstone:** stone shaped like toad, or coming from head of toad (browny grey). **71 infant:** reference to sharp-edged silver coin to cut ligament of tongue-tied infant? **83 errors:** wanderings. **90 caul:** portion of foetal membrane over child's head at birth; denominated (*enstyled*) lucky against drowning. **98 comply:** embrace. **101 spinner:** spider. **111 straiter:** very narrow.

H444 title: *Peculiar*:   H336, title. **3 circum-mortal:** soul.

H449 *To Groves* 6 complaints: laments. **8 rind:** bark. **15 fillets:** headbands. **23 Phillis:** Thracian princess, changed into almond tree when lover failed to return; **Iphis:**   killed himself when Cyprian Anaxarete failed to respond to him. **27 myrtles:** H40, 3n.

H575 The Apparition . . . cf. Tibullus, 1.3.57ff. on Venus leading the poet to the fields of the happy dead. **Desunt nonnulla:** some parts are missing. **1 doves . . . wings:** Psalms 55:6, 68:113 (doves also draw Venus's chariot). **6 ambergris: H1**, 8n. **7 transpire:** emit perfume. **8 storax:** scented gum resin from styrax tree. **14 margents:** margins. **25 Musaeus:** semi-mythological poet, supposed son of Orpheus, believed by some to be the author of *Hero and Leander*. **31 Linus:** fabled inventor of the Greek dirge; **Pindar:** the great lyric poet (6th–5th century BC). **35 subject:** themes (see, e.g., **H40**). **36 Bacchanalian:** follower of wine god Bacchus. **40 comply:** embrace (*Ovid* addressed many of his love poems to *Corinna*). **41 laureate: H8**, 5n., **H111**, 8n. **45 Persius:** this Roman satirist (34–62 AD; H conflates him with Perseus, the victor over snaky-headed Medusa) ends a list of Roman writers and satirists (Lucan, 1st century AD, wrote the heroic poem *Pharsalia*). **51–3 Beaumont . . . Evadne:** the dramatic collaborators Francis **Beaumont** (d. 1616) and John **Fletcher** (d. 1625); H refers to *The Maid's Tragedy*, and the music of the planetary spheres. **57 Jonson:** Ben (d. 1637), poet and dramatist; H was one of his followers (the Sons of Ben). **63 prime:** first hour (ghosts could not walk the earth after this time).

H604 His Prayer . . . Jonson **3 old religion:** Jonson's Catholicism.

H617 His Own Epitaph cf. **H306**. **4 buttoned:** with knob on end.

H642 Farewell Frost . . . **2 diaper:** variegated patterns. **5 gems:** buds. **7–8 Daulian . . . sufferings:** Philomel, raped by brother-in-law Tereus, Thracian king of Daulis, was turned into a nightingale. **10 plunderer:** Boreas, the north wind. **19 temper:** balanced resolution. **22 branch of peace:** olive (Genesis 8:11).

H673 title: Denham: Sir John (d. 1669), royalist poet, author of prospect poem *Cooper's Hill* (1642). **3 pean:** gold spots on dark ground (heraldic); or maybe **paean** = hymn to Apollo (**H197**, 83n.). **6 nicely:** refinedly. **12 Maronian Muse:** Muse of Virgil (Vergilius Maro); **buskins: H142**, 15n. and Luke 3:16. **13 rare:** inestimable.

H686 Funeral Rites . . . **10 trental:** elegy; set of 30 requiem masses. **15 lawny: H78**, 1n.

H713 His Return . . . cf. **H77** and **86**. **7 genius: H77**, 2n.

H723 The Genius . . . *House* **4 benison:** blessing (**living water:** John 4:10). **5 strengthening bread:** Psalm 104:15.

H779 Upon Julia's Clothes **3 liquefaction:** (1) becoming liquid; (2) melting of soul through passion. **5 brave:** splendid.

H784 Ceremonies for Christmas **9 spending:** burning. **10 psalteries:** 10-stringed dulcimer-like instrument (biblical). **12 a-tinding:** kindling.

H812 The Mean puns on golden mean (Aristotle's notion of the mid-point as the virtuous balance between extremes), and the middle, harmonising, parts in music (between treble and bass).

H823 To the King Charles was victorious on 31 May 1645. **3 Victory:** anciently winged, dressed in white and holding a palm branch.

H844 To His Book **6 mackerel:** cf. **H5**, and Catullus, 95.8.

H892 Ceremonies for Candlemas Eve Candlemas (2 February) marks the Presentation of Christ in the Temple but, more importantly, the Purification of the Virgin Mary after giving birth (cf. Leviticus 12:4). **H893, 894** are on Candlemas; **H898** on *Julia's* . . . *Purification.* **17 bents:** reeds.

H898 Julia's . . . *Purification* **1 filletings:** head-bands. **6 candid:** white. **8 decurted:** curtailed. **11 Hymen:** classical god of marriage, invoked in marriage songs (*epithalamia*).

H910 Upon Ben Jonson cf. **H575**, 57n. and **H604, H911**.

H911 An Ode for Him **5–6 Sun** . . . **Tun:** London inns. **12 Or:** either. **17 talent spend:** Matthew 25:14–29 (parable of the talents).

H952 On Himself **1 Weep** . . . **light:** Ecclesiasticus 22:11. **3 Or:** either. **4 Benedicite:** Bless ye [the Lord]; the opening of the canticle *Benedicite, omnia opera Domini* in the Anglican Order for Morning Prayer ('O all ye works of the Lord, bless ye the Lord').

H1026 title: a **distaff** was a cleft rod around which wool or flax was wound. **Saint Distaff's Day** (7 January, the day after Twelfth Day (or Epiphany)) marked a return to mundane toil after the Christmas revels. **6 tow:** coarse flax fibres. **7 plackets:** petticoats.

H1028 title: *Thamesis*: Thames. **3 reiterate thy strand:** rewalk your shores (and the London street near the river so named). **22 naiades:** female river deities.

H1128 On Himself 2 myrtle: victory; love (**H40**, 3n.); immortality (because evergreen).

H1129 The Pillar of Fame according to George Puttenham, *Art of English Poetry* (1578), 2.12, the pillar shape represents constancy, magnificence and rest. **2 Out-during:** outlasting; echoing Horace, *Odes*, 3.30 (and cf. **H376**).

Noble Numbers

N6 Mercy and Love cf. Psalms 36:6–7; 57:1–3 (wings, mercy, justice).

N38 Upon Time a Herbertian poem. **11 pay again:** repay.

N41 His Litany ... Holy Spirit a supplication to the Holy Spirit in its traditional role of Paraclete or comforter. **15 on the lees:** has run out. **21 passing-bell:** bell rung at hour of death to obtain prayers for the **parting** (departing) **soul. 22 Furies:** the three ancient goddesses who prompted the consciences of offenders. **25 tapers ... blue:** the sign of unfortunate ghostly presences. **46 opened ... sealed:** Revelation 5–8.

N47 A Thanksgiving ... for His House cf. **H723. 11 Low ... porch:** common emblem of humility. **22 unchipped:** unbroken; **unflayed:** not nibbled at (by mice, etc.). **28 pulse:** beans, lentils, etc.: i.e., frugal fare. **31 worts ... mess: worts** = general term for vegetables or pot-herbs; **purslane** = common purslane, a pot-herb and salad herb; **mess** = servings. **39 wassail: H1**, 3n. **42 soils:** manures.

N53 To Death 7 bit: morsel, mouthful (at Holy Communion). **9 don ... love:** Isaiah 61:10. **11 gird my loins:** cf. Ephesians 6:14.

N95 Another Grace ... 2 Heaving: lifting. **3 paddocks:** frogs; toads.

5 benison: blessing.

N102 title: a carol for epiphany, 6 January (the appearance of the star to the magi: Matthew 2); possibly recalling Prince Charles (**H213**). **Whitehall:** Whitehall Palace. **3 Lily . . . among:** Song of Solomon 2:16 (referring allegorically to Christ). **21 several:** different. **22 wassailing: H1**, 3n. **23 treble honours:** gold (for **kingship**); myrrh (for Mary, **queen** of heaven; and Henrietta *Maria*); frankincense (also connected with Mary).

N121 title: Bellman: (1) night-watchman, who called the hours; (2) man who announced a death and call for prayers. Cf. Matthew 25:13 (Christ comes at midnight: 'Watch therefore, for ye know neither the day nor the hour wherein the Son of man cometh'). **6 session:** sitting (at court): i.e., Last Judgement.

N128 title: White Island: (1) land of the dead; (2) lost paradisal land to which man is restored in myth and legend; (3) **White** (fortunate: **H77**, 11n.) **Island** suggests fortunate isles, identified with the far western Hesperides; also (4) England (Albion, the white land). **10 sincere:** pure. **11 Candour:** brilliant whiteness; innocence; **lustre:** brilliance; renown. **20 Attending:** awaiting; expecting.

N129 To Christ **2 balsamum:** aromatic healing ointment; cf. Spenser, *Faerie Queene*, 1.11.48 on the **tree** of life (Christ) with the salvific balm flowing from it. **4 sovereignty:** kingly power; the utmost efficacy.

N153 title: see Christ as bridegroom at Matthew 25:1–13; Luke 12:36.

N181 Tapers L. C. Martin (ed.), *Herrick: Poetical Works* (1956), p. 574 cites J. Gregory, *Notes and Observations upon some Passages of Scripture* (1648), Ch. 22 on funeral tapers as emblems of the soul 'not quite put out' and 'gone to walk before God in the light of the living'.

N219 Another **2 predestination:** Anglican Articles of Religion, #17: 'Predestination to life is the everlasting purpose of God'; formed by grace in the image of the second Adam, Christ, we may undo the inherited sin of Genesis 3.

N228 To Keep a True Lent **12 A . . . sour:** Isaiah 58:5. **14–16 wheat . . . soul:** Isaiah 58:7. **17–19 to fast . . . hate:** Isaiah 58:4. **20**

circumcise thy life: as a sign of putting off the old Adam (Deuteronomy 10:16, Romans 2:29). **21 heart grief-rent:** Joel 2:13.

N231 Clothes for Continuance **1 garments ... evermore:** the garments of salvation of Isaiah 61:10 (cf. **N53**, 9n.). **3–4 Which ... cloth:** Matthew 6:19–20, Luke 12:33.

N248 Coheirs paraphrasing Romans 8:16–17.

N249 The Number of Two **1 dual number:** God's failure to announce his 2nd day of creation 'good' (Genesis 1:8; contrast 1:4, 10, 12, etc.) was linked by St Jerome with the Pythagorean/Platonic association of two with evil and division (H. C. Agrippa, *Three Books of Occult Philosophy* [1651], 2.5). **3 several:** individual. **4 curious operation:** ingenious work.

N251 The Rose **2 St Ambrose ... thorn:** St Ambrose (4th century), *Hexaemeron*, 3.11 (for whom the rose signified martyrdom).

N263 Good Friday ... **1 Put off ... purple:** Mark 15:20, John 19:2. **3 Thine ... come:** John 13:1. **11 stick:** the reed of Matthew 27:48. **12 scurf and bran:** scum and coarse men. **19 Roscius:** celebrated Roman actor (d. 62 BC). **29 passion:** suffering on the cross; overpowering emotion. **30 period:** consummation; acme; death. **34 tree:** cross (cf. **N129**). **37 laws of action:** decorum governing part played.

N269 To His Saviour's Sepulchre **13 diaper:** covering of flowers: cf. **H642**, 2n. **15 Panchaia:** fabulous island east of Arabia famed for jewels and incense. **16 Arabia:** also known for its incense. Cf. the spices of, e.g., Luke 24:1.

N271 His Coming ... Sepulchre **2 Is ... gone:** Matthew 28:2–3, Mark 16:3–5 (which also have the **angel**). **6 vanquish hell:** the harrowing of hell is in the apocryphal Gospel of Nicodemus and the creed.

N272 The last poem in *Noble Numbers* **2 ARCHĒ ... TELOS:** in Greek in the original. **Archē** = beginning; **telos** = end, recalling Christ as alpha and omega, first and last at Revelation 22:13 (cf. 1:8).

Everyman's Poetry

Titles available in this series **all at £1.00**

William Blake
ed. Peter Butter
0 460 87800 X

Robert Burns
ed. Donald Low
0 460 87814 X

Samuel Taylor Coleridge
ed. John Beer
0 460 87826 3

Thomas Gray
ed. Robert Mack
0 460 87805 0

Ivor Gurney
ed. George Walter
0 460 87797 6

George Herbert
ed. D. J. Enright
0 460 87795 X

Robert Herrick
ed. Douglas Brooks-Davies
0 460 87799 2

John Keats
ed. Nicholas Roe
0 460 87808 5

**Henry Wadsworth
Longfellow**
ed. Anthony Thwaite
0 460 87821 2

John Milton
ed. Gordon Campbell
0 460 87813 1

Edgar Allan Poe
ed. Richard Gray
0 460 87804 2

Poetry Please!
Foreword by Charles
Causley
0 460 87824 7

Alexander Pope
ed. Douglas Brooks-Davies
0 460 87798 4

Lord Rochester
ed. Paddy Lyons
0 460 87819 0

Christina Rossetti
ed. Jan Marsh
0 460 87820 4

William Shakespeare
ed. Martin Dodsworth
0 460 87815 8

Alfred, Lord Tennyson
ed. Michael Baron
0 460 87802 6

R. S. Thomas
ed. Anthony Thwaite
0 460 87811 5

Walt Whitman
ed. Ellman Crasnow
0 460 87825 5

Oscar Wilde
ed. Robert Mighall
0 460 87803 4